FIDDLE
TRADITIONS

A MUSICAL SAMPLER FROM THE PAGES OF *Strings* MAGAZINE

Twenty five tunes in Bluegrass, Country, Irish, Cajun, Swing,

and other traditional styles, including guidance on how to play them.

Visit Hal Leonard Online at
www.halleonard.com

In Australia Contact:
Hal Leonard Australia Pty. Ltd.
22 Taunton Drive P.O. Box 5130
Cheltenham East, 3192 Victoria, Australia
Email: ausadmin@halleonard.com

STRING LETTER PUBLISHING

EXCLUSIVELY DISTRIBUTED BY

HAL•LEONARD®
CORPORATION
7777 W. BLUEMOUND RD. P.O. BOX 13819 MILWAUKEE, WI 53213

Introduction

Fiddle Traditions offers a look into the multi-faceted world of fiddle playing. Chapters on history, technique, style, tradition, and personalities have been collected from the pages of *Strings* magazine in this fun and informative guide. Filled with musical examples, practice suggestions, and resources for further listening and study, both the novice and veteran fiddler will find in its pages inspiration and practical playing tips. What is the difference between a fiddle and a violin? Turn the page to find out!

Contents

Fiddling is another language and immersion is the best way to learn.

-Donna Hebért

The Reel Deal   1

TWELVE QUESTIONS VIOLINISTS ASK ABOUT FIDDLING

By Donna Hebért

HOW MANY TIMES have you heard someone (perhaps yourself) ask, "What's the difference between a violin and a fiddle?" Beyond the short answer, "spelling," this age-old conundrum invites the ponderer to step beyond stereotypes and assumptions, and to explore music's many meanings. I've encountered the question many times myself. I began as a classically trained violinist, then switched to playing folk music in my twenties. Since then I've taught fiddle at universities, dance camps, and ASTA and NCOA summer camps, as well as at my own In the Groove Workshops and Groove Camp in Amherst, Massachusetts.

Some fiddlers say that the only way to learn fiddling is to hang out and jam with fiddlers, preferably primary sources. It's what the vast majority of fiddlers past and present have done. Others say they've learned most of their repertoire from recordings, while some even learn exclusively by reading. Still, jamming remains the prevalent way of sharing fiddle music with others, and jam sessions are cultivated carefully in communities to maintain this opportunity. Dances (contra, square, Cajun, step, clog) are what fiddling is designed to support, while jams are the ideal setting for actual learning.

There are as many styles of fiddling as there are communities with fiddlers in them, and each regional music has a physical and cultural home. The music fits and describes the place it's played in: the people who play it, the kind of community it is, even the climate!

Be forewarned: After a lifetime of consciously not tapping your feet when you play the violin, it will start to creep back in when you play fiddle tunes. This is perfectly normal and nothing to be alarmed about. It means you're hitting the groove, the place where the music flows like honey from your fingers. Welcome to fiddling. Here are twelve questions that classical players frequently ask about fiddling, and yes, even some written examples to help you make the connection.

1. How does fiddling differ from classical music?

Beat, beat, beat! Most classical music has a stronger accent on the downbeat, while fiddling accents the upbeat for dancers.

Example 1

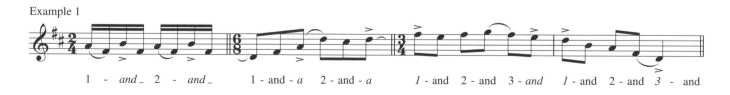

Regional or ethnic fiddling styles use different left- and right-hand techniques to produce authentic sounds, with beat placements and degrees of swing changing from one style to the next.

Fiddle music evolved for dancing, and improvisation and spontaneous composition are the heart of fiddling. Jazz players compose a new melodic line over the chord changes. Fiddlers use the bow and left-hand ornaments to drum a new rhythm over the melody, accenting key parts of the dance with licks, drones, and dynamics, since dancers will use the tune to tell their place in the dance.

Fiddling is an oral tradition. Fiddlers learn hundreds, even thousands, of tunes, almost entirely by ear and in a variety of keys and modes. We learn from other musicians at jam sessions, and from recorded and (sometimes) printed sources. Most classical players use printed music to train the ear, which kicks in when sight-reading the music. But you can't learn fiddle rhythms or styles from written music; you must hear them first. Fiddling pedagogy asks you to hear all the layered parts of a phrase—melody, beat placement, left- and right-hand ornaments, dynamics, chord changes, and other moving lines—and then try to reproduce exactly what you hear.

Playing for dances is fiddling's main function, but jam sessions are the important forum for learning style and for transmitting repertoire and fiddling culture. We learn to play with others at the jam, flowing with the group beat or groove. We create medleys, and arrange tunes creatively on the fly. At "slow-jam" sessions, we play tunes at a slower speed to allow everyone to grab the basic tune, then gradually speed up to a dance tempo: 115–130 beats per minute for hoedowns, hornpipes, and reels in 2/4; jigs or marches in 6/8; and marches in 4/4.

2. Why does fiddling sound so scratchy and out of tune?

There is no universal performance standard in fiddling, nor a universal scale, because scales and standards are culturally relative. We bend notes, raise a scale degree by several cents, and generally emphasize groove over a flawless tone. What you'd call "scratchy fiddlers" are likely to be what fiddlers call "primary sources." We revere these ancestors and tradition-bearers, often trying to emulate their styles. Tommy Jarrell is a primary source among southern old-time fiddlers, and Franco-American fiddler Louis Beaudoin is always in my head when I play French-Canadian tunes. This imitation is done with the utmost respect, even reverence, for the source, hearing beyond limited technique or the infirmities of age to their rhythms, creative variations, and the soul they put into their playing.

3. Why aren't you playing what's written down for the tune?

Published fiddle music is usually only a skeleton of what we play, often lacking bowings, dynamics, ornaments, variations, or even chords. Tunes are usually written unswung, with one full repeat of the melody line (usually two eight-bar phrases repeated; once through most square and contra dances). Variations, beat placement, and bowing syncopations are implied, and change with style. Most of this "performance practice" couldn't be read by the majority of fiddlers. Defining techniques are learned as part of a style, and applied to the tunes as a spoken accent is to a language.

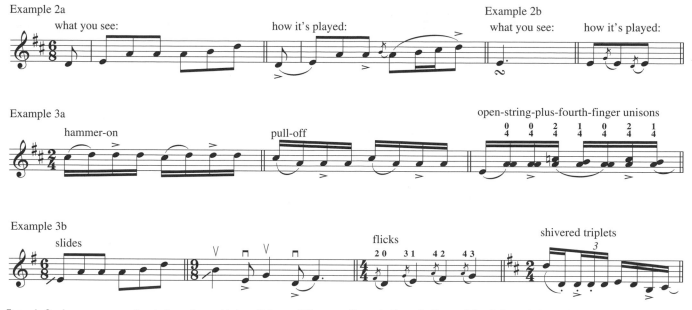

Example 2a

Example 2b

Example 3a

Example 3b

Example 3a shows ornamental techniques from old-time, Cajun, and bluegrass. Shown in Example 3b are slides, flicks, and shivered triplets (borrowed from older piping styles) that appear in Irish, Scottish, and French-Canadian fiddling.

4. Why does it feel like I'm bowing everything backwards?

Maybe you are! Some tunes play easier with an up-bow on the downbeat, reversing what you may be used to. The bowing pattern may even reverse the next time we play the phrase. We may end up bowing a phrase in both directions, producing the same rhythmic accent both ways. Driven up-bows are also common in some styles, while other styles slur across the beat and bar lines for more syncopation. We follow the groove and accent it, regardless of bow direction.

Example 4

5.

In this French-Canadian phrase, accents on driven up-bows create syncopation, almost "ghosting" the note between the two up-bows.

Why don't you use all of your bow?

It's a misconception that fiddlers don't use the whole bow. Regional styles change and vary. Some use long, fluid bow strokes (Texas, Cajun) and others use short, repeated bow strokes (Cape Breton, French-Canadian, and some southern old-time styles). Many fiddlers work off the balance point of the bow, using the weighted center for power and mobility. A player who favors the tip might compensate by choking up on the bow hold to shorten the stick length.

6. What's that rocking thing you keep doing with your bow?

Usually it's a shuffle. Shuffles accent the offbeat for natural syncopation. The basic shuffle forces an offbeat accent in 2/4 (see Example 5). We can create different rhythms by slurring notes together over a two-bar phrase, often across the bar lines and beats. There's a "split bowing" shuffle with two notes slurred, two notes separate, over a pattern of four notes. The Georgia shuffle is a three-slurred, one-separate bowing rhythm that can pop the offbeat out like an elbow in the ribs.

Example 5

bowing: short   short   LONG   short   short   short   LONG   short

Practice this basic shuffle pattern with separate short and long bow strokes to develop a feel for accenting the offbeat.

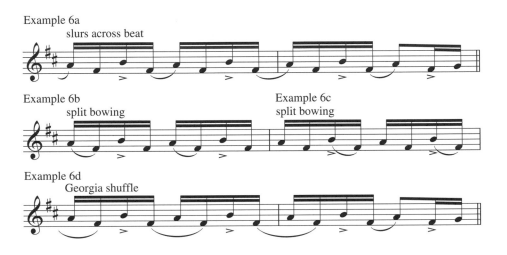

Example 6a
slurs across beat

Example 6b
split bowing

Example 6c
split bowing

Example 6d
Georgia shuffle

7. What about dynamics?

Usually the focal point of the tune is played louder, while some notes are played softer, or even ghosted. Dynamics within a bar punch the offbeat like a heartbeat or breathing—soft, loud, soft, loud. One approach is to play a double-stop drone from the harmony on the offbeat, as in Example 3a.

8. Don't you ever get sick of playing the same thirty-two bars over and over again?

We don't play them the same way over and over. Once you learn the ornaments in any style you'll be able to vary the melody authentically in that style. We also play medleys of tunes for fun and to avoid repetitive-use injuries. Variations begin on the second or third repetition, and then we might vary the rhythm under the tune a little. It's always moving somewhere, never static.

Example 7
melody:

variations:

9. What about vibrato?

You won't hear it much. Most reels are full of sixteenth notes played at 120 beats per minute, with no time for vibrato. You might use it in a waltz, but all ornaments in any style are subordinate to the rhythm. If there isn't room for the ornament "in the groove" we lose the ornament rather than lose the beat.

10. How do you set up, tune, and hold your instrument?

Most modern fiddlers have their instruments set up much like a violinist's. Some fiddlers let the bridge do the work of playing adjacent string drones, filing the top of the bridge's curve down a bit. We may also keep a second instrument tuned to an open chord, say A–E–A–E. In A–E–A–E you can play either in A minor or A major, or both. Many traditions (Southern old-time, Cajun, Scandinavian, and French-Canadian) have tunes that require retuning to A–E–A–E for tunes in A, A–D–A–E for tunes in D, and A–E–A–C♯ for A major. Our fiddling postures are personal, based on physique and inclination (and yes, sometimes ignorance), and often dictated by the rigor of the style we're playing. You'll see many variations on bow and instrument holds.

11. I can already play the violin. How long will it take to learn to fiddle?

First, it's important to recognize the fiddling stereotypes lurking in your subconscious. A common one is the assumption that because "it's almost all in first position, it should be easy, and besides, I can play already." You probably have more left-hand chops than most fiddlers, and are able to read almost anything with facility and speed. But don't underestimate what fiddlers do. How many ways could you rearrange the notes in four or eight or sixteen bars of music at 120 beats per minute, playing the tune authentically with good timing and ornaments, creating tiny rhythmic variations with each repetition yet never losing the outline of the melody, never playing it exactly the same way twice, keeping a rocking offbeat going all the while changing tunes and keys in medleys and arranging them intuitively, all without using sheet music?

Fiddling is another language and immersion is the best way to learn. Find a style you love and learn everything you can—tunes, harmonies, rhythms. Listen repeatedly so your fingers can catch minute changes in rhythm and melody. When you learn any tune the first time, you imprint it, so aim high and learn from the best. If possible, find a mentor you can play with regularly, and learn enough tunes to be able to play in a jam session. Keep a music notebook and write down every tune you learn, noting bowings, suggested harmonies, licks. At the very least, keep a recorded journal and a tune list.

12. Why should I learn fiddling at all?

There are two compelling reasons to learn and teach fiddling in schools and private studios. First, it satisfies all ten of the MENC National Standards for music educators: a) singing music, performing on instruments alone and with others, a varied repertoire of music; b) performing on instruments, alone and with others, a varied repertoire of music; c) improvising melodies, variations, and accompaniments; d) composing and arranging music within specified guidelines; e) reading and notating music; f) listening to, analyzing, and describing music; g) evaluating music and music performances; h) understanding relationships between music and other arts, and disciplines outside the arts; i) understanding music in relation to history and culture; and j) integrating dance with music.

Second, how many of your string students will make it into an orchestra, teaching, or solo career as an adult, or even grow up to play in an amateur chamber group? Don't you want them to have as many opportunities as they can to become lifelong musicians? Besides, you never know where the next Mark O'Connor or Natalie MacMaster is going to come from. Maybe one of your students?

For the classical violinist, vibrato is as unconscious as breathing, but the traditional fiddler views it as an ornament.

-Pat Talbert

Bridging the Gap Between Classical and Traditional Music 2

By Pat Talbert

I HAVE PLAYED classical music for twenty-three years and have worked to master the art of Scottish fiddling for nearly fifteen years. Last winter, I was invited to demonstrate Scottish fiddling in a series of educational concerts given by the local symphony orchestra. During the concerts the children in the audience, caught up in the spirit of strathspeys and reels, began to clap along. Any artist who performs Celtic music will affirm that this is the highest compliment listeners can pay; it assures you that you have successfully conveyed to them the infectious energy of the music.

In the last tune of my set I deliberately picked up the tempo, but the audience continued clapping its original beat. This is a common occurrence with Celtic music audiences, not one to get upset about. I simply played on in my new tempo, not fazed by the audience's slower pulse. On leaving the stage, I was elated at the audience's enthusiastic reaction and the orchestra was too, or so I thought. Later that day an orchestra friend came up and commiserated with me, saying in a distressed tone, "I felt so sorry for you, how could you ever keep up the performance with that distracting beat in your ear?" Her statement underlined for me just how differently a classically trained violinist and a traditionally taught fiddler hear and respond to the musical world that surrounds them.

Most people are aware that differing approaches to music listening and performance exist. Still, my friend's comment that morning showed how vast the distance is between classical and traditional musical disciplines and how difficult it can be to bridge the chasm separating them. This is not to say that it cannot be done. There are players who do it admirably, but they are exceptions. As a player with a foot in each camp, I hope to shed some light on how these approaches differ and offer suggestions on how to narrow this gap and how each can better appreciate the other's musical philosophy.

Most listeners recognize "classical music" when they hear it, even if they can't verbally define it. The term "traditional music" is harder to come to grips with. Over the centuries, traditional music has grown more out of the oral tradition, has been more closely linked to the populace than to gentility, and has been nourished in less formal atmospheres than classical music. Some critics dismissively label traditional music as "easier" than classical music, but in fact it has its own artistry and subtleties that make it as devilishly difficult to master as any violin concerto.

Although I am using here the broad term "traditional fiddler," there are many different regional fiddling styles, such as old-time, Celtic, bluegrass, klezmer, and Texas swing. Each of these styles has its own sub-genres—for example, in Celtic playing there are Scottish, Irish, Breton, Canadian Cape Breton, and other styles.

Let's consider the basic traits found in the classical orchestral violinist versus the traditional fiddler (note that I will oversimplify a bit here, for the purposes of illustration). The orchestral violinist is a highly skilled musician who is the product of years of rigid training, and who is expected to have achieved complete mastery of the instrument's technical demands. These include difficult fingering patterns, agility in various positions on the fingerboard, and an endless variety of bowing techniques. Perfect intonation is an important goal. Also, the orchestral violinist consciously works to blend his or her instrument's voice into that most elusive entity, the unified section sound. The focus is on merging with one's fellow players. The classical musician is trained to follow an external pulse or rhythm given by a conductor's baton; this often includes learning beat anticipation or delay. One must be a master at reading printed notation quickly and repeating back extended passages of music on demand—music written by someone else. It is often considered vital to possess the finest instrument and bow that finances allow.

The traditional fiddler is often the product of years of training as well, but the structure of the tuition is less rigid. "Technical mastery" means something quite different; the fiddler may never surpass the fingering competency or bow-manipulation techniques of a second-year violin student. He or she also rarely, if ever, moves out of first position on the fingerboard; the music seldom demands more advanced techniques. The fiddler strives to play a melody clearly, with good (not necessarily perfect) intonation and, most importantly, with a strong, unmistakable rhythmic pulse. Bow use is, in the main, detached and energetic, though it may not produce as much sheer volume as the classical violinist's. Bow work and melody mesh together to underline the all-important pulse in the tune. A fiddler nurtured in the oral tradition may not be able to read music; most fiddlers over the past three hundred years could not. Instead, tunes and techniques were taught through ear training and repetition, which are still the fundamental methods today. The fiddler learns to hear a melody and play it back, then to improvise and expand on the tune's original form, a theme and variations of sorts. To play a melody identically several times through is considered boring. Blending is not important; individuality is prized and encouraged. And the instrument and bow are usually inexpensive.

I have seen players from both sides of this discussion be dismissive of the other. Classical violinists are notoriously disdainful of their traditional cousins who play out of tune, have horrible tone, and could not follow a conductor if their lives depended on it. Traditional players often scorn their classical cohorts who can't learn a melody by ear, have no improvisational skills, can't change keys while playing, and "can't keep a beat in a paper bag." Of course, many players on each side appreciate the complexities of both types of music.

This article is for the classically trained player who is interested in making a transition into traditional music. This involves what many violinists view as a desertion of basic skills. Vibrato is a prime example. For the classical violinist, vibrato is as natural and unconscious as breathing, but the traditional fiddler views vibrato as an ornament to be used sparingly, if at all. It's difficult for the violinist to understand this, because the use of vibrato is so deeply ingrained—but it's an absolute must in order to play traditional music and be accepted into these circles. I can't count how many times I've heard an enthusiastic violinist try to join a music circle, only to spoil it with the constant use of vibrato.

Another concept that must be modified is playing in tune. Today's classical music is stringently tied to the concept of the well-tempered scale and standard pitch determined by A440. But quite often traditional music utilizes the older, natural harmonic scale, in which all intervals are not equal; in fact, they can be adjusted as the player chooses. Classical musicians find it extremely difficult to accustom themselves to playing "out of tune," and some never get past this stumbling block. While not all traditional playing styles use this alternate scale, anyone who wants to play traditional music well must be able to adapt to this convention when it appears. When in Cape Breton, Nova Scotia, home to an exciting and popular style of fiddling, I quickly noticed that the scale players used was definitely "out of tune," but that everyone played it exactly the same way.

It's common to see traditional American fiddlers' right hands gripping the bow several inches above the frog, or the heels of their left hands collapsed against the back of the instrument neck. Although this is not the most efficient way to produce tone, the traditional fiddler manages to create the music he wants, regardless of personal technical quirks. Also, the fiddler may or may not have a clear, centered instrument tone; its presence or absence is generally not a cause for worry. An awful lot of "bad" fiddling habits can add up to a rich, vibrant music experience. The credo: "If it ain't broke, don't fix it."

The classical player must learn a new set of skills to become a welcome member of this community. Fundamental is the ability to hear a melody and play it back accurately. This is a technique that can be learned, though some lucky souls are born with this gift. Most classical players find it mystifying, because they are generally taught to be dependent on printed music from early childhood (Suzuki method notwithstanding). But countless fiddlers through the centuries have played music their entire lives without ever seeing a sheet of printed music.

Cultivating this aural learning involves such things as learning to distinguish between the actual notes of a melody and the ornamentation added by the player. This is no mean task, especially since an artful player will never play the same ornaments twice in a row. For that matter, mastering the various types of ornamentation and learning their appropriate uses in a certain style requires years of devotion. But the melody itself can vary, also. Thus, the player learning a tune must be able to hear several variations and distill the basic melody from which all versions derive.

It's vital to understand the centrality of rhythm in traditional music. Players establish a beat, then maintain it solely through eye contact and body language. The fiddler is often the leader of the group and must be both the melody and the rhythm player; classical violinists are usually concerned with melody only. The fiddler must maintain a rock-steady beat while simultaneously overlaying the filigree of an improvised, ornamented melody.

The ability to translate a melody rapidly from one key to another is an integral part of many traditional styles. For example, an old-time music circle might start a tune in D. After a few repeats of the melody, a musician yells, "Let's go to G!" and everyone automatically changes key at the top of the next repeat. Shortly after, another voice cries, "Go to A!" and the shift occurs again, effortlessly, with no break in the circle's musical continuity. This spontaneous key-changing, which is so natural for traditional players, baffles those unaccustomed to it. It is accomplished by the practical application of standard music theory and intervallic memorization. While the classical player has a much more conscious grounding in music theory, the fiddler has learned it through constant hearing and repetition of it in performances. The traditional player has also learned melodies through a keen awareness of the tunes' intervals, rather than a visual prop on paper. It is easier and faster to shift these intervallic relationships onto different scales than it is to reposition notes mentally on a staff. The violinist has the knowledge to effect such key changes; it's simply a matter of becoming comfortable with a totally different approach.

As I stood fiddling onstage during that week last winter, something else struck me powerfully, the different audience-artist dynamics of classical and traditional performances. Classical musicians in general are inculcated with the idea that they are to be "heard and not seen" onstage; orchestras strive to let the music speak for itself. Thus there are such formal conventions as wearing black and reducing onstage physical activity to the fewest motions necessary.

The traditional musician works in a far less formal atmosphere, and very often actively works to establish a personal rapport with the audience. Indeed, many of the greatest traditional players deliberately cultivate a stage persona through which to connect with the audience. Whenever I perform traditional music, I take every opportunity to talk with the listeners, to draw them in. Yet in those educational concerts I was struck by the looks on my classical colleagues' faces; they registered amazement that someone from their ranks had learned to put aside that carefully nurtured anonymity and take on an individual, informal demeanor before an audience. If only they could share the joy it brings me!

The worlds of the classical violinist and the traditional fiddler are not so far apart as many people believe. Each has a long, rich cultural history; each deserves respect from the other. Classical violinists may find that they have some technical and intellectual "unlearning" to do in order to join the ranks of traditional players; fiddlers should refrain from disdain and impatience toward classical players trying to develop an appreciation for traditional music because both styles embody admirable aspects of human experience, and both bring joy to listeners the world over.

We fiddlers don't pay much attention to how we're playing; we're just concerned with the what of what we're playing.

-Richard Greene

Birds of a Feather 3

BLUEGRASS AND CLASSICAL STRING STYLES ARE CLOSER THAN YOU MAY THINK

By James Reel

IT'S BEEN A long time since bluegrass musicians had to overcome their unfair image as genetically challenged hicks flailing at fiddles after going out to shoot a squirrel for supper. Great bluegrass fiddling, as everybody has finally realized, takes considerable smarts and skill. In some camps, it's still considered a totally separate world from that of classical violin playing: different repertory, different styles, different techniques, different mind-sets. Yet that's not entirely the case, as you can learn by listening to any Mark O'Connor CD or chatting with veteran fiddler extraordinaire Richard Greene.

Although he started taking standard classical violin lessons at age five, Greene switched to various kinds of folk and popular music in high school. During the 1960s he played with such diverse groups as Bill Monroe's Blue Grass Boys and the progressive rock act Seatrain, and did a lot of studio work in Los Angeles. Since then, he has performed with leading country, rock, and pop artists, and has developed a significant reputation of his own as a virtuoso bluegrass musician.

"Bluegrass and classical music meet at what I think of as the operating manual on how to play the violin," he says. "The fiddle and the violin are the same instrument, and you need to know how to operate the equipment. That's where the nexus is. How far that connection goes is up to the individual player. I made a conscious decision to expand the possibilities of bluegrass fiddling in every way possible."

So Greene's arrangements of bluegrass tunes introduce such classical preoccupations as left-hand pizzicato, ricochet bowing, and more subtle and extensive use of double- and triple-stops and minor seconds.

"You can know nothing and be a successful bluegrass fiddler," Greene acknowledges. "My idol, [Kentucky Colonels legend] Scotty Stoneman, had the most horrible technique imaginable. He grabbed the bow with his fist like an axe handle, and he played only with fingers two, three and four, but with the most powerful technique I ever heard. Also, between the bottom and the side of his fiddle there was a hole big enough to put a magazine through. The equipment was faulty, the technique was weird, but the sound was incredibly focused; the music was *inside* him."

Yet while working in the Hollywood studios, Greene says he was "blown away by other string players noodling on classical pieces during the breaks." He resolved to bone up on proper classical technique and explore the repertory. He bought a copy of Ivan Galamian's *Principles of Violin Playing and Teaching*. Between ages thirty-five and forty-five he independently worked on the Galamian method, learning proper bow grip (and eliminating his horrible calluses) by studying the photos in Galamian's book.

Richard Greene

Still subject to terrible pain from his improper technique, Greene studied with Glenn Dicterow, then concertmaster of the Los Angeles Philharmonic, whose advice completely eliminated his physical problems. "Symmetry, balance, and gravity; that's the answer to pain," he says.

Getting a Trademark Sound

Today, Greene says, "I do tons of teaching in both directions, helping dyed-in-the-wool classical players who are trying to get that bluegrass sound, and helping fiddlers who want to win contests. The first thing I do with fiddlers is show them the pictures in Galamian's book, have them stand at the mirror and imitate that, and then I show them scales.

"Improvising depends on knowing where all the notes are in all the keys. If you're playing in a particular key, how will you know where the notes are if you can't play scales? So I have my students play all the major scales in broken 3rds in first position, for ten or eleven minutes every day. But I don't let them go on to the next key unless they're in tune. Do those scales after you do your usual first position work to avoid injury and pain."

"The first level of practice and development is practicing the first position, which can handle all your fiddling needs. You can do three-octave scales in first position. But that doesn't mean you have to stop there. If you're scared of going beyond first position, just think of second position as the key of C or F; that'll dispel the early pain and horror."

Once his students are familiar with where all the notes are, Greene gives them books with double-stop exercises, like Josephine Trott's *Melodious Double-Stops*.

"That book, coincidentally, uses bluegrass double-stops," he notes.

Working with classically trained adult violinists who want to develop an idiomatic bluegrass style can be even more of a challenge than instilling basic classical principles in his fiddlers.

"One of my students runs a classical violin conservatory, and she has all the technique in the world, but it's baffling to her how to make these bluegrass sounds," he says. "I've been with her a couple of years now, and she's finally ready to do her first bluegrass concert. We've worked on inflection, bluegrass gesture, and the idea of the sound swooping a certain way, which is utterly nonclassical.

"We've worked on radical bow grips that are in direct contradiction to classical training, but let you do wonderful things. And we've worked on the chopping technique, a musical noise you cannot do with the traditional bow grip; it's something I believe I invented in the 1960s that's very prevalent now.

"The fiddler usually knows this stuff, almost instinctively, but it's hard work for a classical player. We fiddlers don't pay much attention to *how* we're playing; we're just concerned with the *what* of what we're playing, and we do it as loud as possible at all times. At least we did back when the microphones weren't good in rural gigs, and we had to be heard over banjos and everything else. With the instruction I finally got, I learned that you can project very well without having to play so loud all the time, and without ruining your body to do it."

This is something of a new concept in bluegrass, Greene says. "You get a lot of variety of dynamics in classical music, but you don't usually hear crescendos and sforzandos and pianissimos in bluegrass unless you come to my concerts. I fill the music up with dynamics."

A good example of the way Greene melds classical technique with bluegrass style is his arrangement of "The Beaumont Rag," published in his book of exact transcriptions of all the violin solos on his CD *The Grass Is Greener* (Rebel, 17140).

"The 6ths in bars 1 and 3 require a powerful left hand," he says. "I think of 6ths, when they run like that, as a classical idea. But you need a bluegrass attack, from off the string; as you hit the string, start the glissando. Then, to handle those double-stops in bar 20, you need to practice your scales. Practicing scales in 5ths is a great way to develop a bluegrass sound.

"In bar 56 you've got those high chords, and when you go up that high you're really bringing classical music into bluegrass, because bluegrass doesn't normally find itself up there. In bars 68 and 69, there's fifth position C major stuff, and in 70 and 71 I take it up even higher, which is something you find in concertos.

"I like the idea of doing variant chromatic patterns, like in bars 74 and 75, as opposed to the trick of randomly letting your hand slide down. I was interested in precision chromatic movement there. And then you've got the octaves from bar 81 onwards. Scotty Stoneman did a couple of octave things, but I do them all over the place."

Greene hastens to point out that no fiddler *has* to use any elements common to classical music, any more than a classical player *must* master bluegrass idioms. But it was through learning as much as he could from both worlds that Greene developed his own rich, unique style.

Greene CD cover

The Beaumont Rag

Traditional
Arranged by Richard Greene

After Banjo Solo:

...when you are playing a fiddle tune you should be free to focus on the melody.
-Julie Lyonn Lieberman

Solving Technical Fiddle Riddles 4

PROBLEMS AND SOLUTIONS

By Julie Lyonn Lieberman

IRISH, OLD-TIMEY, bluegrass, Cajun, and swing fiddle styles all share certain technical commonalities: the keys tend to stay primarily in G, D, A, and E; the bowing arm must stay particularly fluid and be able to cross back and forth between the four strings quickly and cleanly; and the player needs to be skilled at accentuating notes within each phrase as well as using certain key fiddle bowings. There are also different types of slides and embellishments native to each style, but they will not be addressed here.

Fifteen years ago, when I first started teaching privately, I only had my classical and jazz training to refer to when a fiddle student approached me for technical assistance. I'd picked up fiddling through years of performing at folk festivals and didn't know how to teach it. I started off with a didactic approach, assuming that the basics are the basics no matter what the style. But I gradually learned that this is only true if the player wants to develop a technique that will work for all styles of music. If the musician wants only to play fiddle music, learning all twelve keys, shifting up and down the fingerboard, and mastering as many types of bowings as possible just isn't as pertinent as it would be, say, for a jazz player. I also found that certain technical changes in hand position were inappropriate because fiddle music doesn't require the same sounds or moves as classical or jazz.

Although fiddlers have learned by ear for centuries, if you understand a few basics of anatomy and the physics of violin playing, your learning process can move ahead faster than if you wait for the hand to catch up with the ear. Over the years, I've gradually developed a body of right- and left-hand warm-ups as well as mental exercises for my fiddle students. These warm-ups are designed to help players isolate and master the types of challenges that come up in fiddle repertoire. They're based on the idea that when you are playing a fiddle tune you should be free to focus on the melody. If you choose a warm-up that prepares you for a particular tune, then your mind and body will do what you ask much more readily when you move on to the tune itself. Etudes aren't the answer, because not all fiddlers can or want to read music, and most classical etudes don't really address the technical requirements of fiddle music. And fiddlers who do read music usually become too focused on doing so to make the direct mental-physical link necessary to master a tune. When the student is having trouble playing a given tune, whether with physical coordination, phrasing, or memorization, I've discovered the use of "site-specific" exercises to be most beneficial in facilitating immediate improvement.

Here are some of the most common problems fiddlers tend to have, along with pointers and exercises to help solve them.

Too Much Bow Length

Many fiddlers equate speed with effort and inadvertently use too much bow length, particularly while playing fast. Since the only way to get a quality sound when using too much bow length is to move the bow out over the fingerboard, this offense can easily be detected by the amount of rosin you find on the fingerboard. As you speed up, try to use less hair, center the bow between the bridge and the fingerboard, and relax more. Try to use the down bow on each string crossing as an opportunity to drop your arm weight into gravity, thereby giving your muscles constant relief rather than constant contraction, which impairs movement.

Improper Hand-Arm Coordination Crossing Strings

Some players try to initiate fast movement from the wrist. The wrist muscle is extremely weak compared to the forearm; this makes detailed control much more difficult and can cause problems such a carpal tunnel syndrome and tendinitis. I use two terms to describe the primary movements of the arm during string crossings: pump and pivot. While the note-to-note movement should be a push-pull motion powered by the forearm, the upper arm acts like a pump, rising and lowering, to move you from string to string. The exception would be if you were bobbing between the same two strings for an entire passage (such as in the beginning of the B section of "Devil's Dream"). In that case, place your upper arm so that your bow is resting on both strings, keep your upper arm still, and pivot your forearm from the elbow. Practice isolating each movement using short repetitive bows to develop control.

Holding the Fiddle Awkwardly

Many fiddlers tend to hold their instruments against their chests, rather than on their shoulders. This locks the left elbow into one position and forces the hand to operate at a difficult angle, reducing the forearm's ability to rotate and line the fingers up perpendicular to the fingerboard. It also forces the bowing arm too far back; unnecessarily engaging the right shoulder muscle for string crossings. Use a shoulder rest to free the left hand from the responsibility of holding up the fiddle and increase the mobility of the left arm. Choose the most comfortable shoulder rest for your body type by visiting a string shop and trying out the various models.

Uneven Rhythm

Many fiddlers tend to speed up inadvertently on the easier passages and slow down on the difficult ones. Try using a metronome at a slow speed to even everything out, and then gradually, notch by notch, increase the speed. If you start to play out of tune or tense up on certain passages, come back a notch or two until your movement is fluid and tone and pitch are restored.

Below you will find some warm-ups specific to the challenges of the tune "Devil's Dream." All of these exercises should be played slowly first, and then gradually sped up.

Since the tune is in A major, start by familiarizing yourself with the A major scale. Make sure you can play the two-octave scale in tune, knowing the names of the notes as you play them.

Exercise 1

Now let's add some fiddle bowings. The biceps muscle is weakest when it is extended. Play in the middle of the bow where the natural weight of the bow can produce a good tone with the least amount of effort. This position keeps the bowing arm at a right angle, which uses the biceps muscle most effectively.

Exercise 2

Exercise 3

Develop the shuffle stroke by playing it first on each note of the scale, then practice it with open-string double-stops.

Exercise 4

Try to play the double-stops evenly while crossing strings.

Exercise 5

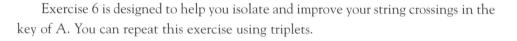

Exercise 6 is designed to help you isolate and improve your string crossings in the key of A. You can repeat this exercise using triplets.

Exercise 6

For intonation problems on a single-line tune, practice some of the passages as double-stops. Tunes that actually do use two-finger double-stops (as opposed to a fingered note against an open string) can be practiced by tuning the lower note first and then adding the upper tone.

As you play the tune, first try using separate bows, and then apply each of the fiddle bowings to the A section. In the B section, practice the difference between pumping to cross strings and pivoting. Ultimately, you will want to place your forearm between the A and E strings (as if you were going to play a double-stop) and pivot from the forearm, using small bows at the middle of the bow. You can refer to the unit "Six-fold Memory" in my book *You Are Your Instrument* for memorization techniques to help you learn the tune.

Devil's Dream

Bluegrass and Double-Stops   5

THREE VARIATIONS ON "TAKE THIS HAMMER"

By Stacy Phillips

FOR THE VIOLIN, bluegrass is one of the world's greatest styles of music. The fiddle has been a featured instrument in its seminal bands, and the style requires a high level of technique. Tempos can be blistering, with frequent passages or even whole solos of slippery, sinuous double-stops.

While open string drones were often used in the old-time music that is a direct precursor of bluegrass, it was not until the late 1940s and early 1950s that double-stops were fully integrated into country fiddling. This time period, coincidentally, also witnessed the creation of bluegrass as a separate category of country music. Benny Martin and Dale Potter were the most influential early exponents of this style, while Vassar Clements, Richard Greene, and Bobby Hicks are noted for continuing to explore the outer reaches of note combinations.

Many classically trained players have difficulty in learning the ways of an improvised music like bluegrass because they lack experience in thinking chordally. When improvising, you must be simultaneously conscious of your solo on two levels: Is your melody coherent; and how does your melody sound when played over the accompanying chord structure?

Becoming familiar with double-stops is one way of beginning this process. Since bluegrass uses relatively few chords per tune, and since these chords are not highly embellished, it is a relatively simple place to begin. You need to have some knowledge of chord structures in order to make intelligent choices of harmonies. Notice how some double-stops herald imminent chord changes, and how they alternate between the tension of relative discord and restful consonance.

For demonstration purposes, I have chosen the medium-paced folk tune "Take This Hammer," giving you the basic tune and three variations in different keys. "Take This Hammer" has been recorded by several bluegrass groups, most notably Flatt and Scruggs and the Foggy Mountain Boys. Play the basic melody at ♩ = 88–100.

In the following discussion of the solos I use Roman numerals to designate chords, and Arabic numerals for individual notes. Do not confuse statements about intervals between notes with intervals between chords. A dominant seventh chord contains the major triad plus the ♭7 of the chord root. (So E7 is made of E–G♯–B–D). My analyses of the notes are in relation to the accompanying chord, not the parent scale. So in measure 3 of the basic melody, the G♯ is considered to be 3 of E7, not 7 in the key of A.

All notes connected by a slur should be played with one bow stroke. Unless otherwise indicated, bluegrass is phrased very legato. One reason for this is that the mandolin and banjo, the other typical bluegrass lead instruments, have very little sustaining power. The fiddle's ability to hold notes offsets this and contributes to this music's version of a "wall of sound," a continuous sheet of musical noise from the ensemble.

The diagonal arrows indicate short (usually not more than a half step), fast slides. The pitch at the beginning of a slide has no duration. The arrowhead indicates whether the slide is up or down. Jagged lines signify a slide between two double-stops that both have prescribed durations. These are also done quickly. Do not change fingering or bow direction during slides. Short slides are usually fast, but you should be able to control a wide range of lengths and speeds of glissandos. There is a certain amount of swaggering in this sort of approach. An attitude of looseness of interpretation requires a sure inner sense of the pulse. You can arrive at a note a bit late or early if you always know exactly where the center of the beat lies. The bowing patterns are suggestions. There is no one correct way to phrase this music. One factor is the tempo: the faster the music, the more slurs. Too many slurs, though, remove the rhythmic punch that well-placed bow changes, which are often on weak beats, can deliver.

The solos follow the melody only approximately. The variations are typical of bluegrass sensibility, as is the fact that the harmony fluctuates between being above and below the lead line.

Take This Hammer

Traditional
Solos by Stacy Phillips

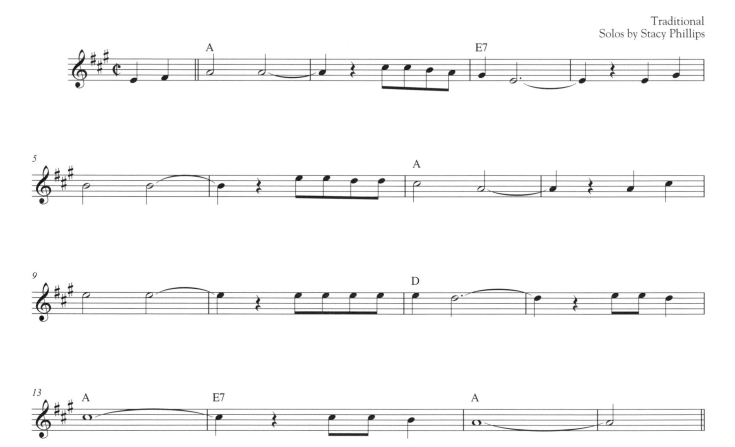

Solo 1

First up is the fiddler's best friend, the key of A. The first solo has a full panoply of double-stop intervals. Most are major and minor 3rds, but there are unisons and 2nds (measure 1), 4ths (measure 9), 5ths (measure 13), 6ths (measure 14), and a 7th (measure 10).

Measures 2-3 contain a I–V chord-connecting lick, beginning with the 1/6 of the I chord (A/F#), moving chromatically to the 5/3 of the V (B/G#). I have made these chord transitions obvious to acclimate you to listening for them.

Of special interest is the way the ♭7 and 9 chord notes are used to prepare a chord change up a 4th. For example, in measures 5-6, first a ♭7/5 (D/B), then a 9/♭7 (F#/D) lead to a resolution of the V to the I (here E7–A). Since the interval between I and IV chords is also a 4th, bluegrass fiddlers regularly alter the I from major to dominant, to allow the same sort of connecting licks. In measures 9 and 10 the ♭7 is held over a moving line and finally resolves in measure 11. A jazz pedagogue might say that the I (here A) has been made the V7 (A7) of the new temporary key of D.

On the other hand, the ♭7 of the D chord in measure 12 is used as a blues effect, not as in classic western harmony. Rock and roll, bluegrass, and swing are three types of music that occasionally switch from classic harmony to blues in midstream.

The one-finger double-stop in measure 13 is a typical attention-grabbing harmony, as is the 1/5 dyad in measure 9. The downward slides in measures 5 and 14 need not be a full half step. It is sufficient that a dip in the pitches be clearly audible. Remember that all the slides in these solos are fast.

Solo 2

As in the first solo, I have tried to arrange the double-stops so as to make the chord changes obvious. Measure 6 illustrates the bluegrass cliché of going from the 3/1 (here F♯/D) chromatically down to the 9/♭7 (E/C). Again, in measures 9-10 the ♭7 is used to prepare a I–IV progression.

Measure 13 has another I–V connector, the 5/3 of the I chord (D/B) moving down chromatically to the ♭7/5 of the V chord (C/A).

Solo 3

The key of B is generally viewed with some trepidation, but since several of the top bluegrass vocalists favor it, fiddle players have developed comfortable ways of dealing with five sharps. The basic ploy is to clamp your first finger over F♯ and B on the top two strings. It acts like a guitar capo. You can leave it there for the first five measures of this solo.

Notice the use of the open A string over the B7 chord, and the similar use of the E string over F♯7 chords. Analyses of these chord-connector licks will show them to be similar to those in the first two solos. The D♯s are used as blue notes, especially as the ♭7 of E in measure 11, and in measure 14 as an anticipatory ♭3 of the final B.

Since these solos have been arranged to illustrate a variety of licks, they tend to be a bit busy. However, you will recognize some of these motives when you listen to your favorite bluegrass fiddlers.

I still respond to the sound of fiddles making music together with the same child-like pleasure that I did when I first fell under its spell.

-Jim Wood

Triple Play

6

LEARNING THE ART OF THREE-PART FIDDLE HARMONY

By Jim Wood

I'VE ALWAYS LOVED the sound of fiddles in harmony, and since fiddlers have a tendency to cluster together whenever two or more are present, I grew up with this sound in my head. I can look back to one day in August of 1976 at Buddy Spicher's place in Fairview, Tennessee as the beginning of my quest for triple-fiddle ecstasy. Buddy, Merle "Red" Taylor, and Dale Potter (with Bob Wills sideman Johnny Gimble on mandolin, no less) were working up some triple-fiddle material in preparation for Buddy's *Me and My Heroes* album (Flying Fish, 065). This sound generated electricity that helped to define my musical future.

Having four of the most important fiddlers in history as my inspiration, I suppose it was my destiny to love multiple fiddles. Once we've covered some technical guidelines, you also will be sharing in the fun in no time at all.

Oh, and also, you'll look really cool onstage.

Choose Wisely

Audiences and musicians alike revel in the power of a well-executed three-fiddle performance, and my goal is to demystify this practice and facilitate your ability to develop your own three-part arrangements.

First, you need to choose material that's a good prospect for three-part harmony. Rather than trying to list criteria for what works well, I think it's more practical to point out a few problematic elements. Range (the highest and lowest notes of a melody and where they lie on the fingerboard) is the first consideration. The most common type of three-part harmony in American folk music places the melody between a baritone part (the next chord tone below the melody) and a tenor part (the next chord tone above the melody).

The melody must not go unreasonably high and must also leave room for a baritone note below. "Grey Eagle" and "Limerock" are good examples of popular tunes with very wide ranges that would not work well. Classical music, jazz, and hymns, by the way, usually have the melody in the highest voice. Folk musicians call this arrangement "high lead," and while it certainly is an optional approach, it does not produce the characteristic sound of fiddling.

Second, a predominantly pentatonic melody typically does not harmonize well, due to the frequency of parallel 4ths between the melody and tenor parts. A pentatonic melody normally leaves out the fourth and seventh degrees of the major scale, and the smooth effect of parallel thirds is lost. "Sally Goodin" is a perfect example of this style of melody.

Third, some melodies are obscured by harmonies. This is totally subjective, but some tunes simply get buried in a morass of fiddle frenzy and would sound much better if left alone.

Methods of Motion

Next, we need to review some music theory. There are four kinds of motion from one pair of notes to the next: In parallel motion the voices move in the same direction using the same interval; in similar motion both voices move in the same direction but the interval between them changes; in oblique motion one voice moves while the other remains stationary; in contrary motion the voices move in different directions. Contrary motion is the only one that is not common in triple fiddling.

In Example 1, we see the four kinds of motion that are available in harmonization: parallel (1a), similar (1b), oblique (1c), and contrary (1d).

The harmonized scale provides the basic materials from which you can develop solid, clear baritone and tenor parts.

In a major key, the triads built on each successive scale degree are major, minor, or diminished due to their need to reconcile with the key signature.

Example 2 shows that the triads resulting from basic harmonization of a scale—in this case C major—will be major, minor, or diminished, depending on how they reconcile with the key signature.

The first technique for assigning upper and lower harmonies around a melody note is to go to the next highest and next lowest chord tones, if the melody note itself is a chord tone of the current chord. For instance, in the key of E major on the IV chord (A major), if the melody note is a C♯, then the tenor would normally be an E above it, and the baritone an A below.

Example 3a

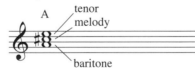

In E major, if the melody note is a chord tone (C♯, the third of the IV chord, A major), use the next chord tone above, E, for the tenor and the next chord tone below, A, for the baritone.

The B melody note on the I chord (E major) would call for an E in the tenor and a G♯ in the baritone.

Example 3b

If the melody goes to B (the fifth of the I chord, E major), try an E above for the tenor and a G♯ below for the baritone.

Although you may sometimes ignore this guideline in a given phrase for stylistic reasons, it will definitely carry you through many situations.

If a melody note is not one of the chord tones of the current chord, then the tenor part will usually be the scale tone a major or minor 3rd above the melody, and the baritone will likely be either the next chord tone below the melody, or the scale tone a major or minor 3rd below the melody.

Example 3c

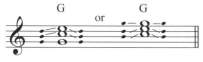

If the melody goes to a note that's not a chord tone (i.e., C or E on a G harmony), try the scale tone that's a 3rd higher than the melody for the tenor, and you may need to experiment to find the best baritone note.

In this case, a little experimentation with the baritone part will be necessary to determine which sound suits your tastes. The same admonition regarding parallel 5ths in classical music generally holds true for triple fiddling in folk music: try to avoid parallel 5ths between the baritone and tenor parts.

Example 3d

Avoid:

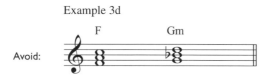

Now we will take a look at a couple of three-fiddle arrangements and point out a few of the finer details. "Glory in the Meeting House" comes from eastern Kentucky. While this mixolydian tune definitely qualifies as old-timey, it has a proto-bluegrass flavor.

Glory in the Meeting House

Traditional
Arranged by James Wood

Breaking Rules

Notice that in measure 1 of "Glory in the Meeting House" we already have violated one of our basic guidelines by using parallel 4ths between the melody and the tenor part. This highlights an important truth about harmony: If you like the way a particular passage sounds, don't worry about whether it's "correct" or not. If Duke Ellington had limited himself to someone's book of rules, he would have sounded like Ray Conniff or Guy Lombardo. The caveat here, though, is that Ellington was utterly cognizant of his every note choice; in other words, know the rules before you break them.

The next point worth noting is that although the bowing for the harmony parts usually mimics that of the melody, either harmony line may benefit from having its own bow pattern to enhance its internal accents and facilitate fluid phrasing (as is the case in measures 4, 7, 10, 11, 13, and 14). Sometimes an awkward string crossing makes a passage inherently weak, and the advantage of using the melody bowing for the sake of continuity is outweighed by loss of rhythmic power and flow. This idea extends even to your note selection; particularly in the baritone part there are certain passages where the best solution to a clumsy harmony part is to leave a note out completely. Measures 7, 9, 11, and 13 demonstrate this. With the parallel harmony of the melody and tenor parts flowing smoothly along, the absence of a baritone note here or there is inconspicuous.

"John Ryan's Polka" is a common session tune from the Irish tradition. This arrangement introduces several new concepts such as unisons, drones, crossed voices, and the implementation of an accompaniment part that doesn't parallel the melody exactly. Two fiddles play the first section of the tune in unison while a third fiddle plays a combination of rhythmic drones and baritone and low tenor parts. (The low tenor uses the next highest chord tone above the melody, but it's played an octave lower; below both the melody and baritone parts.)

John Ryan's Polka

Traditional
Arranged by James Wood

I hope that some of these examples and technical suggestions will help you to discover the sheer delight of wall-to-wall fiddle harmony. In August, 2004, I turned forty years old (I started fiddling at age ten), but I still respond to the sound of fiddles making music together with the same childlike pleasure that I did when I first fell under its spell.

The technique itself can really damage both the music and your reputation if you use it without sensitivity.

-Darol Anger

Get Your Chops Down   7

FIDDLERS—EVEN FIDDLING CELLISTS—CAN LEARN FROM THIS TIME-HONORED TECHNIQUE

By James Reel

SO YOU THINK you're a versatile string player, with good technique and a feeling for rhythms and melodies in different musical styles. But are you versatile enough to play your instrument like a snare drum?

You can do it, once you've mastered a bow stroke called the chop. It's a percussive technique essential to playing solos and backup in bluegrass bands, and useful in a variety of other styles, including jazz and some contemporary art music. Fiddler Richard Greene spread the chop through the bluegrass world in the 1960s and continues to make good use of it in solo work. Violinist Darol Anger is the acknowledged modern master of chopping, but prefers to restrict chopping to accompaniment. Anger's playing is well known through his work with the American Fiddle Ensemble, David Grisman Quintet, the Turtle Island String Quartet, the Montreux Band, and the Anger/Marshall Band. Every year at the Mark O'Connor Fiddle Conference he holds a "chop shop" class.

"The chop plays the same role as the drums and rhythm guitar together," Anger says. "But it can't duplicate an entire drum set, so usually with chopping you're hearing the equivalent sound of the high-hat and the snare part mixed in, which supplies a propulsion that you don't get in any other way, especially in a quartet situation. A lot of quartets now are doing arrangements of pop music and jazz, and without some kind of percussive part it sounds like many of the tracks of the original piece have been removed."

The chop's snare drum effect is obtained by throwing the bow down onto the strings in a controlled way, and quickly pulling it back up. Anger credits Greene with figuring out a way to get an effective but essentially toneless sound on both the downstroke and upstroke. Anger and his Turtle Island colleagues later developed a way to get an honest-to-goodness musical pitch along with the percussive sound on the upstroke.

CHOP ON: Darol Anger

"It's almost a *marcato* kind of sound," Anger says. He has since taught himself to get a pitch on the downstroke, too, which opens up all manner of rhythmic and harmonic possibilities in an ensemble.

But Anger stresses that the basic chop remains a percussive effect used to propel the rhythm in any number of patterns. It's not something you want to overdo, though; he points out that playing too many syncopated beats, chops or otherwise, can confuse the melody players.

"The technique itself can really damage both the music and your reputation if you use it without sensitivity," he says. "The technique is not a toy. This sound, which is very close to noise, needs to be used with restraint to help the groove of the tune. The less you do, generally, the better it sounds.

"In my conception, it's a back-up technique, which means you're not playing louder than the foreground melody; you're weaving into the rest of what's going on, playing just enough to convey the tone quality of the piece and the feeling of the groove, maybe down to just one chop per bar."

Step by Step

Basic chopping isn't hard, but it can be a bit tricky to learn. It's easier if you can start off getting an experienced chopper to demonstrate the move and teach it to you. At least one such expert has put it all in writing: Renata Bratt, author of *The Fiddling Cellist*, published by Mel Bay. She describes a step-by-step process in her new book; the procedure is aimed at cellists, but it's applicable to other string players, too.

Remember that chopping is a bow stroke. It uses a down-up, down-up pattern (down bow is when you pull the bow, up bow is when you push the bow). The third beat of each four-beat pattern is a down-bow gone astray, just a little bit "crunchy" sounding. Try playing straight quarter notes, with the third quarter note crunching down for the chop effect.

FIDDLING CELLIST: Renata Bratt

Bratt offers the following six steps to playing chops:

1. Straighten your bow hand thumb. This is the only time it should ever be straight.

2. Keep your bow very close to the string.

3. Holding the bow, use a slight waving hand motion as if you were slapping a tabletop (but keeping your hand close to the table), or as if you were clapping your hands with your left hand already resting (palm up) on your knee.

4. The chop should occur near the frog.

5. Once your chop makes contact with the string, the chop should also include a slight downward slide away from your body. For violinists and violists the bow will slide slightly toward the fingerboard. For cellists, the bow will slide slightly toward the bridge.

6. The down-bow chop should "stick" to the string (because the weight of your hand is now digging into the string) and make an additional little sound when you let it up on the up-bow.

Listen and Learn

Anger suggests that a good way to learn how to use chops is by listening to the snare drum in first-rate rock and pop bands, and practicing while playing along with recordings. "It's best to play with recordings that already have a good groove, so that you can understand what a good rhythmic feeling is," he says. Bonnie Raitt's recordings have a "wonderful groove," he says, as does Miles Davis's classic jazz album *Kind of Blue*.

Anger recommends Greene's *Sales Tax Toddle* on the Rebel label as an example of the chop as a bravura solo device. To hear it in an ensemble setting, Anger suggests checking out various Turtle Island String Quartet CDs. Among his own releases, he points to his eclectic fiddle-duet album, *Diary of a Fiddler* ("I do a full menu of rhythm techniques, and with only two instruments playing, it's very easy to hear what's going on"), and his new American Fiddle Ensemble disc *Republic of Strings* ("It has my latest and greatest chop techniques, and some brilliant cello playing by Rushad Eggleston"). Both are on Compass Records.

Anger doesn't want to give the impression that he is the be-all and end-all of chopping. "There are endless possibilities here," he says. "Younger players are doing variations of the chop that I could never have dreamed of."

Cluck Old Hen

Traditional
Arranged by Renata Bratt

In this arrangement, chops are represented by the X noteheads. In the A section of the tune, the third cello has the basic chop. Remember to damp the strings with your left hand so that the chop sounds more percussive. Imagine that you're playing the hi-hat cymbal or the mandolin for this rhythm. The second cello is playing a back-up part (not the roots of the chords, but the thirds and fifths). This is another basic rhythmic chop that also helps fill out the harmony. Your right hand should start nearer the fingerboard for the first two beats, and then play nearer the bridge for the chop. (Reverse for the violin and viola, as this is a motion that is started near the body, so that it can move away.)

The B section's accompaniment chops are more challenging. The second cello must be rhythmically steady. If you need to, play a little chop on all of the eighth-note rests. Then the first printed eighth note in each measure would be an up-bow. The motion of your right hand (near the fingerboard for the first two beats, near the bridge for the second two beats of each measure) is the same as that for the A section.

For the third cello part, the written chop is placed closer to the bridge (away from your body). You can also play a little chop (closer to the fingerboard) on the eighth-note rest. Then you'll have a continuous eighth-note beat with chops added. Your right hand should be closer to the fingerboard on the odd beats (1 and 3) and closer to the bridge on the even beats (2 and 4). (Again, this would be reversed on the violin and viola.)

You can combine the chop patterns for the second cello A and B parts to make a nice two-measure pattern.

BASIC MOVE: The chop should occur near the frog (pictured right). Once your chop makes contact with the string, the chop should also include a slight downward slide away from your body. For violinists and violists, the bow will slide slightly toward the fingerboard.

Playing in "deedad" is almost like playing a new instrument.

-Stacy Phillips

Retunings in American Fiddle Music

By Stacy Phillips

UNTIL THE EARLY YEARS of the twentieth century, scordatura, or altering the standard tuning of a violin, was common practice in the folk fiddling of the southern and western U.S. Whether this phenomenon was derived from its limited application in European art music or was reinvented in America is unclear. It was a common practice in Western classical music from about 1600–1750, and it has enjoyed some use ever since. Vivaldi, Biber, Paganini, and Bartók all composed pieces using scordatura. Arabic and Carnatic Indian violin music also commonly use modifications of G–D–G–D (from low to high), with alternate strings an octave apart. And the Hardanger violin tradition of Norway reportedly uses more than twenty tuning variations.

In traditional American fiddle music, the reasons commonly given for the practice are strictly pragmatic. By making the pitches of the open strings members of the triad of the tonic chord (usually the first and fifth notes of the key scale), there is greater resonance, and thus added volume. More important, the player can grab any open string and drone along with the melody to increase his or her sound usually functioned as the sole instrument at square dances, competing to be heard over the shuffling feet of a roomful of dancers.

I have also heard fiddlers say that they enjoyed the physical sensation of the added resonance vibrating against their bodies. And some fingerings are easier when all the open strings fit into the scale and prevalent chords of a tune. But the use of microphones and the popularity of small, fiddle-oriented combos (usually including banjo and/or guitar) that supplied chordal accompaniment decreased the advantages of retunings.

When you do not practice it very often, changing the pitch of a violin can be time-consuming. Most players consider it too much trouble. The majority of old tunes have been adapted, for better or worse, to G–D–A–E, although every old-time, bluegrass, and commercial country violinist knows at least "Black Mountain Rag" and "Bonaparte's Retreat" in their respective scordaturas.

However, there still is a devoted coterie of old-time revivalists who play all tunes in the keys of A, D, and G in what are commonly called cross-tunings. At a typical jam session, they will play a series of numbers (each lasting ten to twenty minutes) in the same tuning and key before changing their open strings for the next round of fiddling. Apparently their violins get used to being pushed and pulled into all sorts of pitch ranges.

The most common variants are: in the key of G, G–D–G–D (from low string to high) and G–D–A–D; in the key of A, A–E–A–E (a transposition of the first variant) and A–E–A–C♯; and, in the key of D, A–D–A–E, D–D–A–D, and A–E–A–D. Other cross tunings include, in the key of E, E–D–A–E and B–E–B–E; and in the key of G, G–D–G–B (a transposition of the second key-of-A tuning). I have chosen three of the most common tuning variations to illustrate the unique tonal potential of scordatura. (I should mention that some players purposely tune above or below standard pitch, while keeping the violin strings in the orthodox relationship of 5ths. Many prefer the mellower resonance of less string tension. But tuning sharp became common bluegrass practice for many years, based on the playing of Bill Monroe's band. This is not retuning in the same sense as the examples given in this article.)

In the piece called "Camp Chase" the standard open-A tuning A–E–A–E is an obvious choice for ease of playing. The same licks can be accomplished an octave apart with no change in fingering. "Camp Chase" can easily be transferred to standard tuning, but the new string alignment creates subtle effects.

Camp Chase

Based on the version by
French Carpenter

The A–E open-string introduction (notated as G–D) rings on for a bit as the high E string is played. The double E that begins section 2 (notated as a double D) is only effective with an open E string in that octave. This kind of double noting is a basic sound in Southern fiddling, and A–E–A–E tuning allows maximum use of it in any key-of-A tune with few chord changes.

The tune's form is quirky, with nine measures in the first section and eleven and a half in the second. With the given accenting in section 1, the third beat can start out feeling like a downbeat, which adds to the eccentric charm. The melody is elusive and need not be thought of as something you can hum, but as a tune with an archaic feel. It would be only slightly misleading to consider this sort of rendition as an Appalachian raga form in a mixolydian mode. Modular pitch contours can be varied as the form is repeated.

Non-pitch effects are equal in importance to the melodic motives. Stress the accents and grind out the bowing. There are many opportunities for mini-slides, which should be thought of as slight blurrings of pitch space as opposed to full-blown glissandos. Try to skate into the first high A in measure 1, the F♯ in measure 7, or the G in measure 19. In the same spirit, do not make a smooth initial attack into the notes. You want to hear the bite of the bow against the string, in the spirit of a plectrum (though not as obvious).

The pulse in the middle of a bow stroke in measure 16 is another Southern fiddle custom. The bowing in the first ending of section $\boxed{1}$ is another nicety in this piece. These variations are interchangeable and can also be played as separate strokes, as in measure 13.

This version is taken from the playing of French Carpenter, an influential fiddler from West Virginia. His grandfather Solly Carpenter is credited with creating this rendition. According to legend, a fiddle contest was held in the Civil War prisoner-of-war camp at Camp Chase, Ohio, and he gained freedom with his reworking of the tune.

French Carpenter played this unaccompanied, so the chords are just my suggestions. His bow strokes were quite short, and typical of many fiddlers from the Upper South, he held the fiddle almost perpendicular to the ground and against the middle of his upper chest, just below his neck.

"Black Mountain Rag" is one of a handful of "showbiz" fiddle extravaganzas. It is not particularly difficult, but the cross-tuning results in many pleasing and slightly exotic double-stops that people who are not fans of fiddling can still appreciate. Many bluegrass fiddlers carry a second instrument tuned in A–E–A–C♯ just to be able to perform this piece at a moment's notice. In fact, this version of the open strings is commonly referred to as "Black Mountain Rag" tuning.

Black Mountain Rag

Based on the version by
Benny Thomasson

This number is derived from an older Alabama tune called "The Lost Child," played in the same cross-tuning. It was reworked in the 1930s by Leslie Keith, an enigmatic fiddler from Tennessee whose playing style was on the cusp of old-time and the more "modern" bluegrass. He called the tune "Black Mountain Blues." Curly Fox, a fiddler with a flair for showmanship, heard Keith play it at a contest, made it flashier, and gave it its current title. Fox recorded it in the late 1940s and, to his amazement, it sold about 600,000 copies. Fiddlers everywhere added it to their repertoires. Gordon Terry, who eventually became a performer on the Grand Ole Opry, says of "Black Mountain Rag," "Ain't no telling how many nickels I put in the jukebox when Curly's record came out. And I played it for six months on the jukebox before I found out he had it cross-tuned."

I have chosen a version by one of the greatest of fiddle-tune stylists, Benny Thomasson. Thomasson, a Texas native, is one of the important creators of the modern contest-fiddle-style that has spread from the Southwest to become a national phenomenon. He once commented on the change of attitude toward retuning in Southwestern contests. "When I was a young fellow, most everybody cross-tuned," he said with a laugh. "But when it got to later years, the younger ones came up who didn't cross-tune. They were raising Cain about it, you know, and stopped all cross-tuning. They didn't want no one else to, because it sounded so much better, you see. Major Franklin [one of Thomasson's toughest competitors] was one that would stomp you to death nearly if you would."

Thomasson plays "Black Mountain Rag" more slowly than he might were he performing it as a show-off number. As usual, he covers a lot of the fingerboard to explore interesting variations, while remaining faithful to the spirit of the piece. Atypically for him, however, Thomasson also employs a bow pattern called the single (or simple, or Nashville) shuffle.

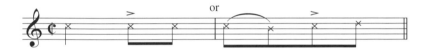

This characteristic Southeastern pattern consists of a long bow stroke (of a quarter-note duration) followed by two short strokes (each of eighth-note duration). The first short stroke is usually accented. The amount of stress varies from Thomasson's subtle style to an almost explosive emphasis (as in the vigorous style of Tex Logan, a mathematician trained at MIT who is also one of the unknown greats of the fiddle-playing world).

The basic melody is stated in section 1 . It exploits the quintessential tonality of this tuning, featuring the droned C♯ string (notated as E). The first four measures are often played while bowing the top two strings to increase the droning. Section 2 features a neat descending double-stopped slide in measure 7, followed by an ascending version in the next bar. The next variation of this part, starting at measure 10, employs a slide to a high A–C♯ harmonic (notated as A–E). This figure can add a satisfyingly frantic edge to this portion.

Tuning to an open chord allows added opportunities for open-string pizzicato, as the two statements in part 3 illustrate. In the first measure of the first variation, measure 15, I like to pick the C♯s (notated as Es) with my left hand and the As with my right. The next motif begins with a difficult series of three-string plucks. I have seen fiddlers accomplish this by quickly grabbing the bow with their mouths (do not bite down) and playing the figure with three fingers of their freed right hands. The first string is played with the middle finger, the second with the ring finger, and the third with the thumb. While the last quarter note of part ③ is sounding, quickly grab the bow and you are ready for more sawing. You might wish to use a fiberglass model for this trick, or even ignore the possibility and discover a more elegant way to play this passage. However, before scoffing, remember that this piece is supposed to entertain the audience. Biting into a flashing neon bow might be just the right touch.

Section ④ employs the bottom two strings, using the G-scale fingering as in standard tuning, but sounding a whole step higher. The added brightness of these strings is another bonus of A–E–A–C♯. The first ten measures are pure simple shuffle, leading into two measures of hokum bowing (also referred to as double shuffle) in bars 33–34. Like the single shuffle, this pattern is made of three strokes. Here the first two are repeated eighth notes and the third is an eighth note on a higher string. (All the strokes are commonly played as double stops.) The three-note pattern sets up a syncopated hemiola. (This device is also the basis for "Orange Blossom Special.")

The order of sections given here is standard, though Thomasson used a slightly different sequence.

"Cruel Willie" is a mournful piece that beautifully exemplifies some of the characteristics of the D–D–A–D cross-tuning (also called "deedad"). In this combination of open strings, the low D is almost always used as a drone, as in sections ② and ③. I especially like the pizzicato of the top two strings against the continuous low drones in the final part.

Cruel Willie

Based on the version by
Howdy Forrester

Try alternate open drones to the ones notated in this version. All the open strings fit the style even if they are dissonant with the chordal accompaniment (for example, the low D over the A7 chord in measure 7). There is a lot of leeway allowed in the amount of slurring, but too much single bowing can take away from the drone effect.

Playing in "deedad" is almost like playing a new instrument. The timbre of a violin can be startling after it has been retuned so drastically. The low D can sound like a harmonious beehive. When you remember that at one time most old-time fiddlers played with the instruments against their chests, like French Carpenter, you can understand how they could appreciate the physical sensation of the added resonance of this scordatura.

This version of "Cruel Willie" is based on the playing of Howard "Howdy" Forrester, and is taken from a very short-lived album released in about 1960, called *Fancy Fiddlin' Country Style*. However, word of mouth and tape trading have tuned it into one of the most famous and respected recordings in fiddledom. Forrester learned to fiddle in his native eastern Tennessee but spent a couple of years in Texas, where he learned many tunes and some of his style from Benny Thomasson. He was one of the most influential breakdown fiddlers in country music.

The tune most often associated with "deedad" tuning is "Bonaparte's Retreat." Here the drones are used in obvious imitation of the skirl of a bagpipe leading a military march. Lyrics were composed for this melody and the song became a hit for several country music performers, including Leon McAuliffe and Charlie Walker.

Bonaparte's Retreat

Based on the version by
Benny Thomasson

Napoleon's adventures captured the imagination of many generations of fiddlers, and the litany of eponymous melodies includes "Bonaparte's Defeat," "Madame Bonaparte," "Bonaparte's March," "Bonaparte Crossing the Rhine," "Bonaparte Crossing the Alps," and even—unbelievably enough—"Bonaparte Crossing the Rocky Mountains." This arrangement is also based on the playing of Benny Thomasson.

Thomasson exhibits some beautiful bow control in the first section, rocking the bow slightly to separate the F♯ quarter notes while keeping the low D (notated as G) sounding continuously. Meanwhile he imparts emphasis to the second and fourth beats to give his playing an infectious lilt.

The melody of measures 3–4, 7, 13, and 14 is sometimes played in octaves, as one-finger double-stops on the bottom two strings. This is the only exception to the droning of the low D string that I know of in traditional fiddling.

The extra measures in the second and fourth repeats of section 2 are a time-filling device, again in imitation of bagpipes. This sort of asymmetry (between alternate repetitions of a segment) is one convention of old-time fiddling.

The first section is somber, while the second should be played more forcefully. The last part is bright, with a defiant air. The long bow strokes throughout this piece accentuate the slurred articulation of a bagpipe. Thomasson ordinarily played saw strokes (one note per bow) with scattered, syncopated accents thrown about. The variations on "Bonaparte's Retreat" and "Black Mountain Rag" show that he had command of the whole range of old-time fiddle techniques.

For American fiddlers, "modal tunes" are those that use a mixture of scales in a way that blurs their harmonic identity as major or minor.

-Stacy Phillips

The Exotic World of Modal Fiddle Tunes

9

By Stacy Phillips

"PLAYING IN MODES" is a phrase that gets tossed around with a remarkable lack of clarity. It appears that classical, jazz, and pop musicians, as well as ethnomusicologists, all have their own definitions. For American fiddlers, "modal tunes" are those that use a mixture of scales in a way that blurs their harmonic identity as major or minor.

The most common variation from the standard major scale among fiddlers in the American South is the mixolydian, the major scale with a flatted seventh step.

Example 1

Modal tunes are occasionally spiced with flatted thirds (the real culprit in the confusion between major and minor) and major sevenths. If enough flatted thirds are used, the scale of the tune approaches the dorian.

Example 2

It is the presence of at least occasional non-diatonic tones that makes this species of traditional tunes especially appealing, at least to fiddle fanatics. Another endearing aspect is the wide range of acceptable accompanying chords. You can get away with staying in the tonic chord for most of these pieces. However, inserting unexpected (usually major) triads makes a piquant aural *frisson* with the melody. The key of A, because of ease of fingering, is the favorite setting for modal tunes. Three examples from the Southern repertoire illustrate typical characteristics.

This version of the traditional tune "Pretty Little Indian" is based on Curly Ray Cline's rendition. Cline has been a fixture on the bluegrass scene for four decades. In the 1950s he played with one of the first bluegrass bands, the Lonesome Pine Fiddlers. For about the last twenty-five years he has fiddled with banjoist Ralph Stanley and the Clinch Mountain Boys, a group that is a bedrock of traditional bluegrass sound. With passing time, Cline's approach has become much simpler and more old-timey sounding, with fewer double-stops and flashy bursts of fast licks than he employed with the Lonesome Pine Fiddlers. But he still has a wacky stage personality as the yokel among yokels. When he solos, he grits his teeth in a grin and literally leans into his efforts, with his left leg bent, his torso leaning sharply to the left and his right leg stretched out as if it were feeling for footing in the dark. The impression is of a fellow who was born on a steep mountain and grew used to this posture to keep his balance on the precipitous incline.

"Pretty Little Indian" is a medium-paced tune meant more for listening than for dancing. The basic scale is mixolydian, and the flatted seventh scale step introduces an A–G–A cadence. In measures 9 and 20, G chords would fit better with the melody notes than chords in E, but I favor the V–I resolution in bluegrass settings. Old-timey bands might prefer to use the G harmony, or simply to stay with the A chord and damn the cadence.

Pretty Little Indian

Based on the version by
Curly Ray Cline

A diagonal line indicates a short, quick slide (more like a finger flick) up to the indicated note. The pitch at the beginning of the slide has no duration. The bow should not change direction during this movement. A squiggly line also indicates a slide without any bow change, but in this case the initial pitch has a definite duration.

In this kind of tune, it is typical to interchange the sixth scale step with the flatted seventh (here, F♯ and G♮), and the second scale step with the flatted third (B and C♯). Additionally, the flatted third can substitute for the natural third; here, a C natural can replace a C♯ and vice versa. So measure 3 might be played as in Example 3, and measure 12 played as in Example 4.

Example 3

Example 4

The venerable age of this tune is also evidenced by the extra measure introduced by the extended Es in measures 7 and 18. Fiddle tunes are always expected to have eight measures per section, so this metric crookedness makes things even more peculiar. (Crooked fiddle tunes are the equivalent of bebop in old-timey music. Aficionados use them to weed out non-initiates from jam sessions.)

The notated accents are not particularly strong and are part of Cline's shuffle bowing (except for the slides from E to D). The first measure of "Pretty Little Indian" and Example 5 both illustrate the single shuffle, the clichéd pattern of Southern fiddling. The accents add a danceable syncopation. Knowledgeable fiddlers would automatically insert the stresses without any need to notate them.

Example 5

or

Another subtlety that is not notated is the uneven phrasing of pairs of eighth notes. An eighth note on a downbeat is usually held a bit longer than one on an upbeat. Example 6 shows the closest approximation in Western notation. Usually, the faster the tempo, the closer to a literal interpretation.

Example 6

or

Adding the previous eighth note to the slur results in the shuffle variation known as the Georgia bow, in which the accent is usually more pronounced (see Example 7). The predominance of these patterns in this arrangement highlights Cline's efforts to sound old-timey, as opposed to more modern approaches to traditional fiddling.

Example 7

In "Abe's Retreat," the major/minor haziness of modal tunes is more apparent. Despite the absence of the major third in the melody, most accompanists would stubbornly play A major triads instead of minor. (There is some evidence that generations of Southern banjo and guitar players refused even to acknowledge the existence of minor chords until after World War II.) However, once your ear accepts the resulting dissonances, the minor tonic chord will sound positively enervated, and a veteran accompanist might gaze upon you with a combination of pity and repulsion should you suggest a minor harmonization.

Abe's Retreat

Based on the version by
Danny Gardella and Bill Christopherson

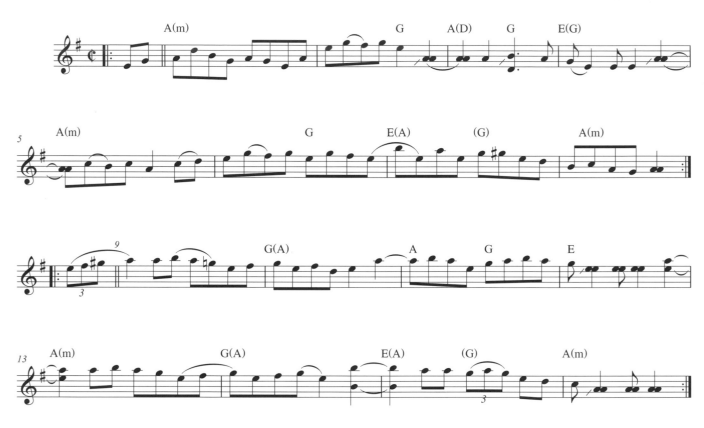

A diagonal line indicates a short, quick slide (more like a finger flick) up to the indicated note. The pitch at the beginning of the slide has no duration. The bow should not change direction during this movement. The capital letters above the staves indicate the chordal accompaniment. Those in parentheses are alternates.

If you find the G♯ against the G chord unbearable in measure 7, either play an E chord through the measure or use the variation in Example 8. The chord choice is an important part of the sound of this tune, so find some pliant accompanist to experiment with.

Example 8

This version of "Abe's Retreat" (also known as "The Battle of Bull Run" and "Manassas Junction") is adapted from the playing of Danny Gardella and Bill Christopherson, two stalwarts of the fiddle scene in the Northeast. (Unlike Curly Ray, they usually play while standing erect, although Gardella has been known to keel over in mid-bow.) The bowing is not as detailed as in "Pretty Little Indian," so feel free to rearrange it. If the triplet in the introductory measure of the second section comes out on an up-bow, cut the slur after the G♯ and play the following A with a down stroke. Play this tune on the fast side.

"Shag Poke" takes the scalar/harmonic confusion, as well as enigmatic titling, several warped steps further. (The name may refer to chewing tobacco, or to some inexplicable Appalachian ritual.) Though the tune opens and closes in G, suggesting a lydian mode, (see Example 9), everything in between hollers A mixolydian.

Example 9

Theory follows practice; so if it sounds good, leave the speculation to someone looking for a thesis topic. I find that hearing the chords is particularly important to the enjoyment of this melody.

Shag Poke

Based on the version by
Pat Conte

The double open-string tones are important though subtle aspects of this style. As in "Pretty Little Indian," give the second and fourth beats of most measures a bit of an accent.

This arrangement is based on the playing of Pat Conte, who specializes in authentic recreations of archaic musical traditions. His ferocious collecting of the associated records and instrument arcana, along with his reclusive lifestyle, fit perfectly with the tenor of this tune.

Texas Hoedown Fiddling 10

BENNY THOMASSON-STYLE

By Jim Wood

ONE OF THE MORE significant developments in American traditional fiddling in recent decades has been the proliferation of the Texas contest style throughout much of North America. In rural Texas, where a strong tradition of fiddling reaches back to the pioneer days, contests have served for years as a spectator sport of sorts for the many folks who play for their own enjoyment. Stimulated by the friendly competition among the best of these fiddlers, Texas contest fiddling has been raised to a well-defined art form in which individuality and sophistication are blended beautifully with taste and respect for tradition.

Without a doubt Benny Thomasson (1909-1984) must be considered the quintessential practitioner and promoter of this style. Thomasson played a major role in transforming the traditional old-time tunes of his father's generation, which usually consist of binary forms repeated with little deviation from the basic melody, into highly evolved arrangements employing sophisticated variations and additional parts. His stylistic innovations have profoundly influenced the art of fiddling in general, and, as in rare and special cases, his technique was the perfect complement to his conceptual creativity. Most importantly, though, his music has that intangible spiritual dimension that makes great music great. Thomasson established the standards by which Texas-style contest fiddling can be judged, and the sheer quality and musicality of his playing ranks him as one of the premier traditional musicians of all time.

Thomasson's style, labeled "progressive" by some folks, is actually rooted very firmly in the old-time dance music he inherited from his ancestors. Many of the tunes he played can be traced to the British Isles or the American frontier, but he possessed the ability to transform the music without disturbing its original meaning. Although he infused jazz and blues elements, they never seemed simply added on; he arranged and improvised variations that grew out of the basic tune in a thoroughly organic fashion. Thomasson seemed able to get inside tunes and accentuate their fundamental substance while remaining completely personal and fresh in his approach. As a result, his music has both the depth and wisdom of tradition, and the vitality and excitement of innovation.

Thomasson's technical facility freed him to explore the higher registers of the violin; his dexterity and coordination opened virtually all options in realizing his musical goals. Never sacrificing the quality of a melodic line for the sake of pyrotechnics, he executed with grace and ease passages of formidable difficulty that his musical ideas dictated with grace and ease.

1980 Old-Time Fiddling Champion, Benny Thomasson.

Thomasson's melodic invention is revealed through even a cursory investigation of his playing. What many folks fail to realize is that the magic, the thing that breathes life into his fiddling, is his bow work. The rhythmic subtlety created by his bow patterns, his choice of slurs and single strokes and string crossings, gives his music a rich and dynamic quality that can best be described as having drive.

"Little Joe," recorded on *Benny Thomasson: Volume One*, highlights some of Thomasson's typical bow work and his melodic variety. This transcription does not show his penchant for elaborate formal developments (as in, for instance, his treatment of "Tom and Jerry" on *Benny Thomasson: Country Fiddling from the Big State*), but it does give insight into his subtle improvisatory skills. He is obviously playing off the top of his head. "Little Joe" was recorded late in his life, and even though he had lost some of his technical precision, he seems to play as freely and creatively as ever. The drive and bounce are also intact, and Thomasson, as always, locks into the ideal tempo (about 110 beats per minute in this case).

Since Thomasson is improvising, the feel of the music can best be understood by listening to his recordings and becoming directly involved by playing along with him. (The next step is to venture out on your own and jam with other players familiar with the style.) But a few helpful words can be said if you do not readily have these options. The rhythm guitar, the most common instrument used to accompany Texas-style fiddling, plays, for the most part, a jazz-influenced bass line on the down beat with a staccato strum of the chord on the backbeat. This creates the swing feel that underpins the fiddle lead. You can go a long way toward achieving this groove by practicing with the metronome on the backbeat (the accents will fall on the third and the seventh sixteenth notes in a measure of 2/4). Start slowly and try to match your bowings to the metronome accents.

Much of the subtlety in Thomasson's playing results from his use of slurs and string crossings that create syncopation against the backbeat rhythmic undercurrent that is always present in his bow hand (an excellent example of this occurs in measure 33). You must remain completely relaxed and not rush any note; a tune such as this derives much of its drive from being laid back. The sixteenth notes have a syncopated feel somewhere between

and

This is easily overdone, so be careful.

Besides the melodic variations and bowing alterations that are obvious on reading through this transcription once, Thomasson also creates color and richness with more subtle techniques. His liberal use of the lydian modality (as, for example, the C♯s in measures 7-8) and chromatic approach notes (measure 62, for instance) gives the melody added brightness and zing. You should, by the way, use all open strings unless the fourth finger is indicated, and you should use no vibrato (this is the general rule for hoedowns). Thomasson's bow strokes also play a large role in the overall effect of his music. In a moderate hoedown tempo such as that of "Little Joe," he employs a stroke similar to détaché, but which has a lot of bounce (sometimes the hair even comes off the string) and which is generated more in the wrist than in the arm. He also uses, as in measure 27, a lively hooked bowing. The dynamics are, for all practical purposes, forte throughout, but slight swells and mute differences from note to note that accentuate the rhythm of a given phrase are quite evident.

I have included a typical set of chord changes in case you have a guitarist or pianist handy. The substitutions in the first part are not written in stone but are what you will likely hear from any Texas-style rhythm player. Do not be alarmed when the melody and the chords seem to bear no theoretical relationship to one another (as in measure 32, when you play a C♯ over a D7 chord); both instruments are going to the same place, even if they take slightly different routes. Somehow the tension and clashes sound wonderful.

"Little Joe" provides an excellent starting place for anyone new to Texas-style fiddling because, even though it is relatively accessible (compared to tunes such as "Sally Goodin" or "Dusty Miller"), it contains many of the outstanding features basic to the style. From no better representative than Benny Thomasson can you learn. His playing not only displays beautifully the technique of hoedown fiddling, but communicates a genuine joyousness and love of life.

Little Joe

As Recorded by Benny Thomasson
(John's BT-48014)

His music formed a bridge from the old to the new and consequently resonated with rural Southerners' lives and times.

-Jim Wood

Modern Southern Fiddling 11

THE GENIUS OF ARTHUR SMITH

By Jim Wood

IN AN ERA when satellite TV has become commonplace, most of us can't recall the days when even a radio was a rarity. Yet it was only fifty or sixty years ago that radio and records first began to permeate my part of the country, Tennessee and the Southeastern United States. The coming of broadcasting transformed our popular musical culture. It introduced local and regional artists to wider audiences, and brought enormous new musical influences to bear from outside. The "country music" of today evolved directly from the music of these radio and recording pioneers.

The fiddle had always been an integral part of Southern music, and the greatest fiddler of that era was a Middle Tennessean named Arthur Smith (1898-1971). Smith transformed the traditional fiddle music of his parents' generation, descended in large part from the British Isles, creating a new and intensely personal style which was more vocally oriented and influenced by jazz, pop, and blues. In many ways, it reflects a special stage in the sociological development of the New South as it entered into the modern era. His music formed a bridge from the old to the new and consequently resonated with rural Southerners' lives and times.

Arthur Smith dominated the stylistic development of an entire generation, and his influence is still indirectly felt through the many popular fiddlers who so thoroughly assimilated certain aspects of his playing. His work has served as a model for amateurs and professionals alike. Having lived my whole life in Middle Tennessee, I have seen firsthand that our regional style owes much to Smith's direct influence, and echoes of his music (both his instrumental technique and his original tunes and songs) are heard throughout country music to this day.

Smith's fiddling caught listeners' attention with its clean, fluid lines and rhythmic aggressiveness. He achieved this combination by employing what the old-timers call the "long bow,"

where the constant shuffle bow pattern so prevalent in string-band music is abandoned in favor of longer and more frequent slurs. (Look at the first line of the "Fiddler's Dream" transcription for a perfect example.) But too many slurs create a weak rhythmic effect, and Smith knew perfectly the trick of strategically placing slurs and single bow strokes into phrases, so as to amplify their intrinsic strength. The result is a flowing, hard-driving rhythm that avoids the stiffness and monotony of using just one bow pattern throughout an entire tune. His bowing style also allowed him to play at very fast tempos without sounding choppy, and this, among other things, excited folks. Many of the younger fiddlers learning during Smith's heyday in the 1920s and 1930s modeled their right-hand work on his smooth strokes.

Smith also led the way in making blues a prominent feature in country fiddling. Many of his original compositions, such as "Florida Blues" or "Fiddler's Blues" (both recorded on *Fiddlin' Arthur Smith & His Dixieliners*), were not blues in the strictest sense of the term, but relied heavily on slides and blues phrasing, especially in medium tempos. He incorporated this blues feeling into virtually everything he played. The two transcriptions contain both very subtle blues, such as the slides in measures 0 and 10 in "Fiddler's Dream," and pure, low-down-and-dirty blues, as in measure 27 of "Sugar Tree Stomp." The minute variations and details of blues are impossible to notate, and listening and imitation are the only ways to a really accurate performance, but in general, the glissando (the F# tied from measures 6–7 in "Sugar Tree Stomp" is a good example) starts approximately a half step below the target in an upward slide and lasts throughout the entire rhythmic value of the note. In other words, you will not reach the actual written note (F# in this case) until the last instant of its notated value, and the slide must remain even and relaxed. You should not take the notation of phrases such as measures 27 and 35 too literally, but be careful to follow the recommended fingerings, even if they sometimes seem unorthodox, in order better to approximate Smith's phrasing. (By the way, use open strings unless otherwise indicated.)

"Fiddler's Dream" and "Sugar Tree Stomp" (both from *Fiddlin' Arthur Smith & His Dixieliners, Volume Two*) are excellent examples of Smith's innovative breakdown style, and each is performed at quite a peppy tempo (140 beats per minute for the former and 130 for the latter). The rhythmic feel of each tune, as with any fiddle tune at these speeds, is very straight-ahead, with the sixteenth notes even and legato. When playing these pieces yourself, try to maintain a rhythmic edge and stay right on top of the beat. As you can hear on the original recordings, Smith sounds very aggressive while avoiding stiffness. If you are not accustomed to this style (or even if you are), start learning these pieces at a ridiculously slow tempo and work your way up while carefully keeping each note (with the exception of the glissandos) perfectly in time. By the time you have gradually attained the desired tempo, you should feel comfortable enough to stay relaxed.

On these recordings, the Delmore Brothers play accompaniment on guitar and tenor guitar, with an alternating bass pattern (root, fifth, root, fifth, etc.) on the downbeat (the metronome click on 1, 2, 1, 2, etc.), and a chord strum on the backbeat (the "ands" in between the clicks); the accent is on the downbeat. This is the standard "oom-pah"-type rhythm, with the guitar or piano or whatever you have available leaning into the "oom."

Play these tunes as many times through as you like; use the coda only when you are ready to end. If you listen to the recordings (and please do), you will hear that these transcriptions have some cutting and pasting with regard to the noting and the bowing; I simply borrowed a little bit from each time through the form in making my transcription. Smith, by the way, very rarely does any out-and-out improvising, and his variations are quite subtle.

Southern fiddling would have inevitably evolved in some direction, but it developed the way it did because of Arthur Smith. His popularity as a fiddler and singer made standards of a substantial portion of his vast repertoire of original fiddle tunes and country songs. (He performed everything from old-timey breakdowns to pop tunes and jazzy rags.) His sophistication, by the standards of country musicians before him, and his incredible imagination and sense of style made Smith one of the all-time greats, and his playing laid the cornerstone for bluegrass fiddling.

Fiddler's Dream

By Arthur Smith

Sugar Tree Stomp

By Arthur Smith

Baroque to Bluegrass   12

A HISTORICAL LOOK AT BARIOLAGE

By Fred Palmer

IT IS A SOUND that belongs unmistakably to the violin: The player changes more or less rapidly from one string to another while alternating between stopped and open notes on two or more strings, building musical interest and with it a unique sense of drive, tension, and anticipation through the alternation of tone colors. The technique is known as *bariolage*, French for "medley of colors." You will find it in such widely disparate musical cultures as Northern Italy in the Baroque, and Appalachia in the mid-twentieth century.

The most familiar bariolage is hard-driving and almost hypnotic in its pacing. But how fast must the string crossings really be? How many of them must occur? Is there any well-defined musical context in which bariolage ought to happen? After examining the use of bariolage in different eras and genres, I have come to believe that it should be viewed in the broadest possible context, allowing for a variety of tempos and formal settings. In my view, it is a technique that may be used to convey harmonic progression, melodic variety, and structural clarity.

Old fiddle tunes and bluegrass compositions abound with examples of bariolage. One version of the well-known "Devil's Dream" uses it in the middle part. The clear implication is that every possible open string must be so played.

A modern bluegrass piece, "Orange Blossom Special," develops this truly fine bit of bariolage, further enhanced by hemiola:

The technique was immensely popular with violinist-composers during the seventeenth and eighteenth centuries. The earliest hint of the style that I have found dates from 1670 in a *Sinfonia* for two violins and continuo by Alessandro Stradella (1639-1682). Soon thereafter, extended passages of the device are to be found in sonatas, partitas, and concertos by all of the principal string writers of the era. Two impressive examples by J.S. Bach utilize bariolage-like figures throughout, namely the preludes of the *Suite No. 6 in D Major for Cello* and the *Partita No. 3 in E Major for Violin*.

Some of the passages from Bach's partita involve crossing three strings and require perfect coordination between arm, wrists, and fingers. A student learning the work should benefit from alternating slow and fast practice, initially playing the notes in various groups of four at the faster tempo, insuring all the while that each note receives its full value. (It has been my experience that the note on the middle string tends to be weaker than the others.)

Such extended usage is rarely seen in works from later periods. It may be worth exploring briefly why this change occurred. Among other ideas, Baroque composers adhered to the Doctrine of the Affections, which decreed that a musical composition, or, more properly, a movement of an extended work, having once established a particular mood or affect, should maintain that mood throughout. Having exposed the listener to the shimmer of bariolage, the composer is more or less committed by the Doctrine to continue.

With that ideal in mind, I began searching for works that utilize bariolage as their main constructive element. One is Fritz Kreisler's *Praeludium and Allegro* in the style of Pugnani, the celebrated Italian violinist and composer whose own style of composition resembled that of Tartini. (For many years, Kreisler managed to pass off this dazzling little piece as his arrangement of Pugnani's original, a ruse he perpetrated on concertgoers several times.)

Written in Baroque style (as envisioned by Kreisler), this work contains several passages of bariolage and closely related figurations. The prelude itself is essentially a magnificently slowed-down version of bariolage.

Allegro

The allegro is built around a lively motive that repeatedly resolves into rapid string crossings alternating fingered notes and open strings. Near the end of the work bariolage is combined with hemiola over a dominant pedal to produce a stunning virtuoso effect.

Here one's sense of the meter can be endangered by the displaced accents. At the same time, the bowing pattern requiring two notes on the E string followed by one on the A can get extremely problematic in a lively tempo. Slow practice in a variety of rhythms seems to hold the key to success.

With the close of the Baroque era, musical ideas underwent profound changes. The Doctrine of the Affections, which supported non-thematic movements and restricted key relationships, gave way to the dramatic juxtapositions of various melodic, harmonic, and technical styles. Instead of serving as the foundation for an entire movement, we find bariolage relegated to a specific use. Key signatures grew more complex, while those that utilize the open strings of the violin became correspondingly less common, so that bariolage became impossible or inappropriate for some pieces.

No composer of his day was more closely attuned to the dramatic capabilities of musical form than Mozart. He utilized symphonic forms in his operas and operatic forms in his symphonies and concertos. He was primarily responsible for the melding of the Baroque concerto-ritornello form (itself an outgrowth of the opera aria) with the newly emergent sonata-allegro from into the Classical concerto form.

The dramatic impact of Mozart's forms arises from the establishment of well-defined sections within the movements of his multipartite works. Each section, every new thematic statement, be it in exposition, development, or recapitulation, is an event. In order to clarify these events, Mozart enhanced the standard harmonic cadential formulas with melodic and rhythmic formulas of his own, choosing from a myriad of figurations. It should come as no surprise that one figuration chosen for a violin concerto was bariolage, which occurs in the *Concerto in G Major, for Violin and Orchestra, K. 216*. There the following passage closes the solo exposition and the recapitulation.

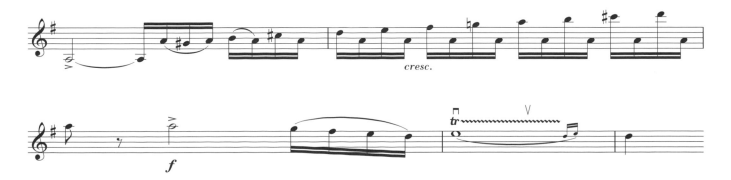

Johannes Brahms envisioned a loftier role for bariolage. Because the technique is, as seen in the examples, closely allied to broken chords, arpeggios, and Alberti figurations, it sometimes matches, in general contour, the frequently used broken chord figures in the composer's keyboard style (the Finale of the *Sonata in G Major for Violin and Piano, Op. 78*, measures 5-14, for example). In the development of the first movement of the *Sonata in D Minor, Op. 108*, however, the principal theme, first heard in the opening measures of the violin, is combined with the piano part of that same first measure into a bariolage figure in the violin, this time over a dominant pedal. The entire development section of some fifty-three measures is structured around this bariolage-like figuration.

molto **p** *e sotto voce sempre*

Bariolage has not been shunned by composers of the twentieth century. Two examples come readily to mind. The first is from the opening movement of Prokofiev's *Violin Concerto No. 1 in D Major, Op. 19*, and the second is a brief but stunning passage from Bartok's *Violin Concerto No. 2*, which utilizes quartertones to extend the already striking color of this style.

From a practical point of view, each passage involving bariolage must be dealt with on its own merits. In general, the practice of double-stops can be used to secure pitches in the left hand, and dotted rhythms in combinations such as long, short; short, long; two long, two short; and two short, two long can be used to facilitate string crossings. For the practice of hemiola with bariolage, such as in the Kreisler, eighth-note patterns can be grouped three-plus-five rather than four-plus-four.

Bariolage has played an equally important role for all the members of the violin family, not only in the solo sonata and concerto literature, but in chamber music, bluegrass, pop, and jazz as well. By learning to recognize it in its several applications and guises, the string player should be able to present more effectively those passages in works where the technique plays a part of the musical fabric.

Cookin' with Cajun Spice   13

PLAY "BETWEEN THE NOTES" TO GET THAT AUTHENTIC LOUISIANA FLAVOR

By Suzy Rothfield Thompson

WHEN I FIRST heard the Balfa Brothers play at a folk festival in the mid-1970s, I fell in love with Cajun music. The sounds emanating from Dewey Balfa's fiddle moved me to tears. I started making trips to Louisiana to visit older musicians there. I would try to imitate their music, but I couldn't figure out why, when I was playing the same melodies (not the same "groove," but that's another story!), the music just didn't have the evocative Cajun flavor that I heard in the playing of the old-timers. Then I learned about their secret ingredient.

It's no coincidence that Cajun fiddle master Dewey Balfa appears alongside chef Paul Prudhomme on travel brochures touting southwest Louisiana as a tourist destination; food and music are Cajun Country's most famous exports. In both arts, attention to detail is vital. To get a truly Cajun-tasting gumbo you need to use spicy andouille sausage rather than the milder kielbasa. Similarly, to produce the exotic flavor that makes Cajun fiddling so distinctive, you'll want to emulate Cajun intonation, even though at first it may sound out of tune to your ears.

Great Chefs

Dennis McGee and Dewey Balfa served up that sound better than just about anyone else. McGee (1893-1989) was one of the first Cajun fiddlers to record back in the late 1920s. He laid down about thirty sides under his own name and recorded magnificent, otherworldly fiddle duets with Ernest Frugé and Sady Courville. He also recorded many sides with the legendary Creole accordion player Amade Ardoin. Like many musicians of his generation, McGee gave up fiddling for years while raising a family. But by the time I met him in 1978, he had started playing again and had even done some touring. He remained an inspiring fiddle spirit right up into his ninety-fifth year.

Balfa (1927-1992) grew up in a musical family in the generation after McGee. Balfa began recording in the early 1950s, and he performed at the Newport Folk Festival in the mid-1960s. At that time, Cajun music garnered little respect in Louisiana, where the nurturing of Cajun culture had been discouraged for years. The Cajun musicians got a tremendous reception from the college-educated folk revivalists at Newport, however, where they found themselves onstage with such icons as Bob Dylan and Joan Baez. When Balfa returned home, he was determined to spearhead a revival of old-time Cajun music, and he certainly succeeded! Because of his tireless efforts, this beautiful music has not only survived, but it's flourishing in the twenty-first century.

DOWN ON THE BAYOU: (l to r) Rodney Balfa, Dewey Balfa, Nathan Abshire, and Basile Marcentel—Basile, Louisiana, 1966

Stay Sharp

The key to creating that Cajun sound lies in playing certain notes sharp. The best way to figure out how sharp is to listen closely to a source recording, but to help you get started, I've provided some visual clues in the transcriptions printed here. I've used up-pointing arrows to indicate notes that should be played sharp and down-pointing arrows for notes to be played flat, and I've placed an "X" over the arrow if the note is very sharp or flat.

In Cajun fiddling, the G on the E string is often played sharp. If the tune is in D, the note will register as a G that is sharp, but if the tune is in A, it will register as a G♯ played flat. Essentially, the second finger on the E string is placed in between G and G♯. The same is true of the second finger on the A string: it's often placed somewhere in between C and C♯. The F♯ on the E string varies: some fiddlers, including Balfa, tended to play this note a bit sharp, whereas others, like McGee, tended to play it a bit flat.

For some examples of the G played sharp, look at "Two Step de L'Anse à Paille." Of course, you should also listen to the source recording from which I transcribed the piece. In this tune, Balfa plays the G consistently sharp, and rather than making it a passing tone, he gives it a prominent place at the beginning of the second phrase. Listen, too, to the way he slides into that G in measure 4, and how he slides out of it in measure 6.

Two Step de L'Anse à Paille

By Dewey Balfa
Transcribed by Suzy Rothfield Thompson

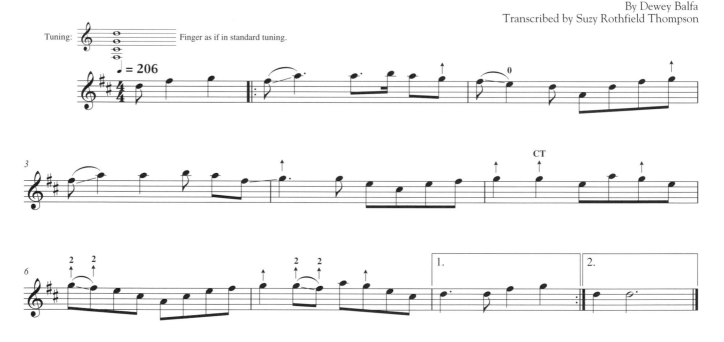

Tune Low

Many Cajun players tune their fiddles a whole step low, that is, F–C–G–D instead of G–D–A–E. The reason for this is the subject of speculation. This dropped tuning might be used to lower the pitch for singing, or to make it easier to use open strings when playing with a C accordion. (The Cajun button accordion is diatonic, providing only the notes of a major scale. C is the most common key for these instruments, although accordions in D and B♭ also exist.)

Still, not all Cajun fiddlers tune low, not even those in the older generation. But it's pretty common, and it gives the music a very characteristic, somewhat hollow sound. Balfa usually tuned low, as did Wallace "Cheese" Read, Canray Fontenot, and Wade Frugé, among many others. When I met McGee in the 1970s, he tuned his fiddle low, too; but on his 1920s recordings, he sometimes tuned low and sometimes to standard pitch. A few older-generation Cajun fiddlers always tuned to standard pitch, even when playing with the C accordion; Lionel LeLeux got some really interesting tonalities that way (especially with the open E string in the key of C.) You can hear his influence in the playing of fiddler Michael Doucet, leader of BeauSoleil.

Note that I have transcribed the tunes as they are fingered, not as they sound on the recordings. So although I have written "Two Step de L'Anse à Paille" in D, when you listen to the Balfa Brothers' recording, it will sound like C because of Dewey's low tuning. Likewise, "La Valse du Bambocheur" is written in A, but the fiddle was tuned a whole step low so it will sound like G. On "La Valse Pénitentiaire" the fiddle is tuned about a half step flat.

La Valse du Bambocheur

By Dewey Balfa
Transcribed by Suzy Rothfield Thompson

La Valse Pénitentiaire

By Dennis McGee
Transcribed by Suzy Rothfield Thompson

Dress It Up

Cajun fiddlers often use slides and single trills for ornamentation, and I've indicated a slide with a diagonal line in my transcriptions. Cajun fiddlers use both upward and downward slides; the latter produces the "crying" sound that is so characteristic of Cajun fiddling. Classically trained musicians can feel odd playing a downward slide because they end up playing a note with the "wrong" finger. There are examples of this in measures 6–7 of "L'Anse à Paille." You'll play the G on the E string with the second finger (as usual) and then slide down to the F♯ with the same finger. The intonation should be sharp all the way through this slide, because all the Gs are played sharp in this piece, and the F♯ should be sharp, as well. This slide should be done fairly quickly; it's just a way to get from one note to the other using one finger.

The trill (marked CT in the music) is a single half-step trill, probably a vestige of the Irish influence on Cajun music. In "L'Anse à Paille," this comes up in measure 5, on the second G. Play the trill as a G to an A♭, or as close to the G as you can get. It shouldn't register as a separate note; you may not even want to put your third finger all the way down on the fingerboard.

Listen Up!

The best way to learn this trill is to listen closely to the way the great Cajun masters such as Balfa and McGee played it. In fact, the key to learning to play Cajun fiddle music (or any kind of orally transmitted music) is listening. Think of it this way: Your gumbo needs to simmer for many hours before it tastes right, and will taste even better if you put it in the refrigerator overnight and reheat it the next day. Similarly, once you've acquired some recording of Cajun music that you like, listen not just once or twice, but over and over again, until you hear the tunes in your dreams. It's also helpful to analyze a transcription of the music, but there's no substitute for repeated listening, preferably over time.

Just as the long simmering and overnight stay in the refrigerator lets the gumbo flavors develop, deep listening over time will allow your brain to absorb subtleties about Cajun music that can never be transcribed.

Listening, Viewing, and Doing

Listen:

The Balfa Brothers Play Traditional Cajun Music, Vol. I and II (Swallow, CD-6011) includes "Two Step de L'Anse à Paille," transcribed here. It also includes a version of "La Valse du Bambocheur."

The Complete Early Recordings of Dennis McGee, 1929–1930 (Yazoo, 2012) features "One Step des McGees" and "La Valse Pénitentiaire."

Cajun House Party, Wallace "Cheese" Read (Arhoolie, CD 415)

Old Style Cajun Music, Wade Frugé (Arhoolie, CD 476)

Under a Green Oak Tree, Dewey Balfa, D.L. Menard, and Marc Savoy (Arhoolie, CD 312)

View:

The DVD *J'ai Été au Bal* by Les Blank, Chris Strachwitz, and Maureen Gosling provides an excellent overview of Cajun and zydeco music.

Do:

Two weeklong music camps offer an intensive Cajun music experience:

Dewey Balfa Cajun-Creole Heritage Week (www.lafolkroots.org) is run by Dewey's daughter Christine Balfa, and offers both spring and fall programs.

Augusta Heritage Center's Cajun/Creole Week (www.augustaheritage.com) takes place during the summer in Elkins, West Virginia.

Good fiddling should have the looseness and spontaneity of jazz as well as the focus and tightness of a Bach partita.

-Jim Wood

The Science of Contest Fiddling

14

By Jim Wood

FIDDLE CONTESTS SEEM to be everywhere these days. Within a two- or three-hour drive from Nashville, a person can go to a competition of some sort on almost every Saturday from April until October; and, from what I hear, a similar situation exists throughout much of the United States. While all the basic regional styles, including Southeastern, Cajun, Appalachian, New England, and Canadian, continue to thrive, the Texas contest style, with its emphasis on more advanced technique and structural development, has evolved during the last two or three decades into something resembling a national contest style. Regional differences are still reflected, even when fiddlers from different states perform the same basic variations to a tune, but the repertoire and approach to form are Texas-style.

Eck Robertson is the most widely recognized of the early architects of the Texas style, but Benny Thomasson and Major Franklin stand as the twin towers of what I consider mature Texas-style contest fiddling (Orville Burns, Dick Barrett, and James "Shorty" Chancellor, among others, have also left a profound mark on this art form). All of these folks, with the exception of the Oklahoman Burns, are Texans. While I have learned much from their recordings (and from a few good jam sessions), I personally owe, as does every noteworthy contest fiddler from the Southeast, a lifetime of gratitude to J.T. Perkins of Arab, Alabama, the man who has given Texas-contest-style fiddling a distinctively Southeastern voice. Already a master of the more straight-ahead Southeastern traditional style, Perkins has adopted the Texas repertoire and approach of adding new parts to the simple (usually two-part) tunes. But his unique variations reflect his creative genius and are no mere imitation of the Texans who inspired him. This is the essence of a true artist, someone who learns and thoroughly assimilates the work of other masters and then transforms it into something new and vital by infusing it with his own personality and vision.

Contests from region to region and also within a given region can vary greatly in atmosphere and type. They can range from pure Texas contest style, with its heavy swing influence; to a modal, mountain style, which might even allow for open tunings (which are usually outlawed); to a bluegrass-flavored competition, at which a category or two of fiddling is simply included in a full day of band, banjo, guitar, mandolin, harmonica, dobro, and buck-dancing rounds. Here in Tennessee I see each of these varieties, but I'll focus now on what someone is likely to find at a typical "contest-style" competition and look at one piece each from the typical tune categories of breakdown or hoedown, waltz, and tune of choice. The National Championship in Weiser, Idaho, requires a tune from each of these categories in six different rounds for a total of eighteen selections. Weiser has so many contestants that it lasts for a full week and has a strict time limit of four minutes for each three-tune round; most competitions are completed in a day or two and have two or three rounds with no time limits. Sometimes scores are cumulative, but more commonly each new round starts with a clean slate, in which case players have to decide whether to use their hottest material to advance past the elimination round and get to the money, or save their best stuff for the finals. Only the experience of such contests can help in these cases.

The same is true for choosing the best possible pieces for any given set of judges. The quality of judging runs the gamut from the best contests with championship-quality fiddlers who can discern the most subtle techniques and artistic interpretations, to the one-horse contests with the local barber at the helm, who knows only three chords on the guitar (assisted by the caller at the community square dance, who does not play an instrument but who "sure does like music a lot"). Keep this in mind and take everything that happens with a grain of salt. While selecting the most appropriate pieces for a given contest might mean holding back with some of the hippest material, highly accomplished contest fiddlers will never lower themselves to playing show cannon fodder like "Orange Blossom Special" or "Listen to the Mockingbird" (these tunes and others like them are normally banned anyway) out of respect for the other good fiddlers and the audience.

The order of performance can, of course, vary according to the circumstances, but more often than not it seems to be: breakdown, waltz, and tune of choice. Most typical breakdowns trace their ancestry either to a reel or a hornpipe (these accompany the dances for which they are named) from the British Isles or from the Southeastern tradition, where white and black musical influences melded into a uniquely American style. "Tom and Jerry" began its life as a two-part hornpipe, but has been transformed into a set piece with loosely organized but widely recognized parts that grew out of the original binary form. Breakdowns are always in 2/4 time and typically work well in the ♩ = 96–132 range; this version of "Tom and Jerry" sounds best at about ♩ = 108–112. The accompaniment plays the basic "boom-chick" or "oom-pah" swing rhythm, with the walking bass line following the chord progression indicated above the melody. (This progression is not written in stone anywhere, and good rhythm players will vary it throughout the piece.) Sections $\boxed{A}$, $\boxed{C}$, $\boxed{E}$, $\boxed{F}$, $\boxed{G}$, and $\boxed{A1}$ have the same basic harmonic structure, and sections $\boxed{B}$ and $\boxed{D}$ also share the same chord changes. The bowing is designed to bring out the swing character of contest-style fiddling, with many of its most typical syncopations, but whether slurring over it or not, the afterbeat (or backbeat) pulse should be felt. Also, with this and the other two pieces, use open strings unless the fourth finger is explicitly indicated; this does much to create the proper rhythmic groove and timbre of good fiddling.

Tom and Jerry

Arranged by Jim Wood

THE SCIENCE OF CONTEST FIDDLING

Choosing Tunes

The following list contains some of the most standard of the standard tunes played in fiddle contests.

Breakdowns
- Sally Goodin
- Sally Johnson
- Grey Eagle
- Dusty Miller
- Limerock
- Forked Deer
- Leather Britches
- Say Old Man (Lady's Fancy)
- Durang's Hornpipe
- Billy in the Lowground

Waltzes
- Gardenia Waltz
- Yellow Rose Waltz
- Chancellor's Waltz
- La Zinda
- Martin's Waltz
- Dreamy Georgianna Moon
- Kentucky Waltz
- Festival Waltz
- Canadian Waltz (Ookpic Waltz or Utpik Waltz)

Tunes of Choice
- Twinkle Little Star
- Cotton Patch Rag
- I Don't Love Nobody
- Jesse Polka
- Clarinet Polka
- Black and White Rag
- Herman's Rag
- Dill Pickle Rag
- Allentown Polka

One comment: I seldom play all the little details of an arrangement the same way twice. This goes not only for minor changes on repeats, but also for an arrangement as a whole. In the actual competition itself, the top-quality fiddlers improvise on the microcosmic level but usually hold to the form and many of the key phrases that they have practiced beforehand; but in the jam sessions off the stage they tend to explore and improvise in a much broader fashion. This is how fiddlers find their style; once some new ideas pop out in a let-it-rip jam, those ideas are collected, taken home, and polished up later for a stage-ready arrangement. This process of using improvisations as the raw material for worked-out variations is different from jazz, where a new creation seems to be the goal of each performance. Good fiddling should have the looseness and spontaneity of jazz as well as the focus and tightness of a Bach partita. It comes from a dance tradition in which it must be entirely self- supporting from a rhythmic and structural standpoint. Wide open jazz-type jamming over the chords does not provide the melodic and rhythmic continuity necessary to keep it in the realm of fiddle music (most contest-style fiddlers enjoy jamming on old swing standards to satisfy the appetite to improvise in this more jazz-like fashion). Also, contest winners must play with the same kind of technical precision and flawlessness associated with a top-notch classical performance. Again, only experience and the chance to play in a good musical scene can define these stylistic parameters for each individual.

"Tom and Jerry" is on anybody's top-five list of contest repertoire, and while less common tunes can be interesting and a nice change of pace, the ability to get up and stand toe-to-toe on the standards with the top players is necessary to earn respect. This tune benefits from the drones in sections $\boxed{A}$, $\boxed{E}$, $\boxed{F}$, and $\boxed{A1}$, and the ringing, open quality of the fiddle in A major; thus the fiddler has the opportunity to jar down and play loud and strong. (The double-stops indicated have one note that is the melody and the other that is a drone and/or harmony; the energy is focused on the melody line and the other note will take care of itself.) This arrangement contains few fancy licks but is designed to bring out an aggressive rhythmic drive—this is what speaks to the listener. Practice it slowly with the metronome clicking on the afterbeat, and then gradually increase the tempo while maintaining that afterbeat accent—a hard-swinging groove is the most important aspect of a good breakdown performance.

Now comes "Rose of Sharon." I have not researched this, but I believe, due to its melodic character, that it has Scottish roots (alternate titles include "Rose of Shannon" and "Rosebud of Avonmore"). A contest waltz should not be draggy and too slow for actually dancing a waltz, but it should be sustained and spacious enough to show off good tone: ♩ = 88–138 or so. I like "Rose of Sharon" around ♩ = 108. Vibrato here must be used judiciously and never on drones or short notes (eighth notes and shorter). Avoid sliding off or into notes, because this creates rhythmic weakness and lack of focus with regard to intonation. In general, you should use slides, glissando, or portamento (whatever term you prefer) sparingly and with intent; slipping and sliding around mindlessly can sound sloppy and obnoxious very quickly. The grace notes provide a much cleaner approach to ornamentation in a waltz. This arrangement is typical in that double-stops are added on the second time through the piece. Everything here is in first position unless otherwise indicated. A good contest waltz must be melodic and must not rely on gimmicks and licks idiomatic to the violin.

Rose of Sharon

Arranged by Jim Wood

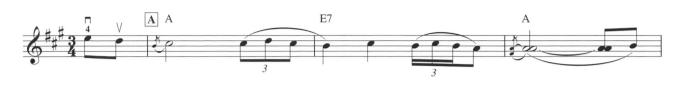

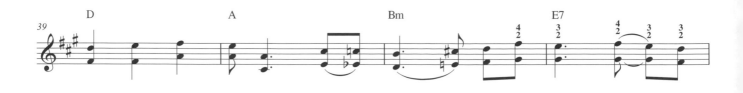

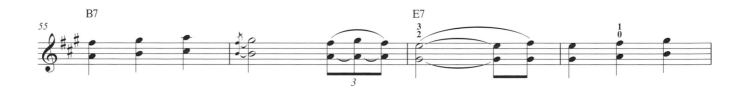

Finally comes "Beaumont Rag." I don't know where this piece originated, but Bob Wills, the king of western swing, certainly had a hand in making it popular. Rags are probably the most common of the various tune-types that fit into the tune-of-choice category (others include polkas, jigs, schottisches, and tunes that don't fit neatly into any of the typical types). They display some common characteristics, such as circle-of-5ths progressions (see measures 14–16 of this arrangement), repetitive three-note patterns (section C), melodies that strongly reflect the dominant seventh chord (measure 1), and the ragtime syncopations of measures 5–7. Rags are slower than breakdowns and sound good from ♩ = 96–112; this arrangement works well at ♩ = 104. Rags also open up greater possibilities than other tune-types for jazz-influenced phrasing (see the last line of section C , for example) and a straight-ahead swing groove. Note that the double-shuffle bowing pattern (also called "hokum" bowing) in the first two lines of section E will be outlawed at many contests, because it can be used as a flashy trick in many tunes in which it would be completely inappropriate; you can simply omit this section if you like.

Recordings

The following albums, featuring some of the great fiddlers discussed in this article, can help beginning contest fiddlers learn the sound and styles of contest fiddling.

Major Franklin
Texas Fiddle Favorites, with Lewis Franklin and Norman Solomon (County, 707)

Mark O'Connor
The Championship Years (Country Music Foundation, CMF-015-D)

J.T. Perkins
Just Fine Fiddling (Davis Unlimited, DU-33007), *J.T.* (Davis Unlimited, DU-33044)

Benny Thomasson
Country Fiddling from the Big State (County, 724)

A Jam Session with Benny and Jerry Thomasson (Voyager, VRLP 309)

Texas Hoedown, with Bartow Riley and Vernon Solomon (County, 703)

Beaumont Rag

Arranged by
Jim Wood

A few things need to be said about attitude. Although this is art and not football, it is still competition, and the best players want to win; pride, as well as money, is at stake. Performing in a fiddle contest is certainly not the be-all and end-all of the complete musical experience; the competitive edge that is necessary for success can be limiting in certain ways. But the flip side is that it can provide energy and focus, bringing a musician into a pure zone in which everything but the tune and the groove falls away. This is an incredible feeling. Judges are listening for good technique, grasp of musical style, and creative variations, but the groove is what grabs people and holds them. Without pushing too hard and sacrificing the subtleties that make fiddle music special in the first place, one must drive it home with authority.

Unsquare Dances 15

By Hollis Taylor

AFTER SEVERAL YEARS of focusing on melodies and harmonies, I recently developed a hunger to concentrate on more complex rhythmic forms in my explorations of fiddle music. I began to collect tunes that had an extra beat or two, an extra bar or two, or just odd forms. In the back of my mind, I longed to stumble on an unknown American fiddle tune in seven, but I didn't hold my breath.

Then I moved to Paris. There I began looking in earnest for that elusive tune in seven, haunting music stores and festivals throughout France. At last I heard about a Parisian bookstore that specialized in Celtic music. I made several unsuccessful trips; it wasn't open every day, and of course not during the generous lunch "hour." But I finally found the store open and, in it, a book filled with Celtic transcriptions including a good number in compound meters. Encouraged by my first score (in two senses of the word), I picked up the pace of my search. A trip to Spain netted some wonderful Basque tunes, including one in 5/8 and another alternating 6/8 with 3/4.

Then a stroll through the cobblestone alleys of Krakow, Poland, a city spiced with Baroque cupolas and church spires, led to one of the largest market squares in Europe. Here, in the center of the old town, I discovered several stores filled with sheet music and recordings of Polish folk music. Inspired, I extended my search to many other European cities and villages. My game plan in each new place was simple: music, museums, architecture, food, and wine. I was not disappointed.

After two years I moved to Budapest, where I took full advantage of the city's plethora of nightly international folk dance clubs, all with live music. I wanted to know how to dance in five and seven and eleven. And, under the still bright guiding light of Béla Bartók, and influenced by my love of American jazz and fiddle music, I began composing violin duos based on these European folk dance tunes in compound meters. The result was nineteen tunes from fourteen countries, every one in a different meter, which I turned into *Unsquare Dances*. Here are two of those tunes, "Fast Forward" and "Sending the Bride to a Stranger's House."

Each piece could use a little explanation. "Fast Forward" was inspired by the Bulgarian *gudulka*, a bowed string instrument that is a distant relative of the medieval rebec. Its small, pear-shaped body is held vertically, supported by a strap (or a well-fed belly). Three strings are bowed and eleven add their voices in shimmering sympathy.

Fast Forward

By Hollis Taylor

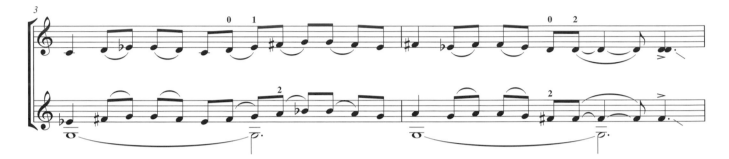

Any ♩ in the melodic line may be ornamented by a turn to the note a half step above it, unless it has a slide marking.
These notes are not important harmonically or tonally, only as rhythmic articulation.

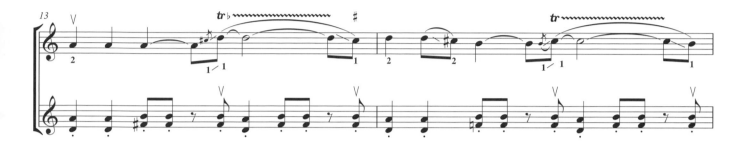

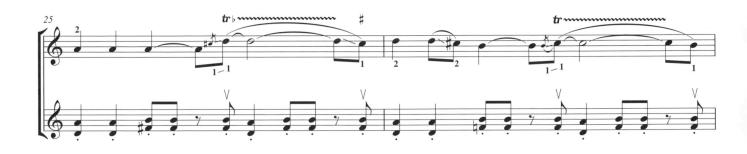

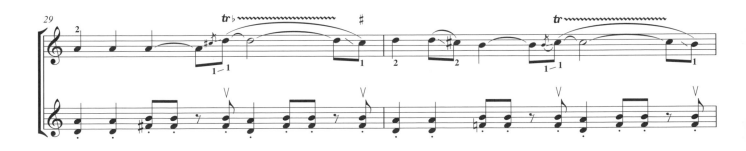

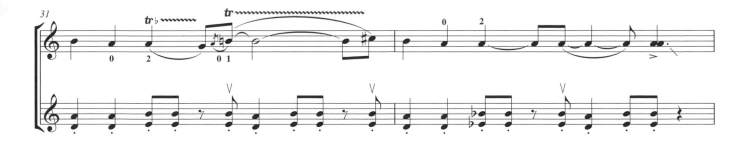

Rhythms typical in Bulgaria are anything but business as usual for the rest of the world. Bartók marveled at their asymmetrical complexity. "Fast Forward" is really in 7/8, subdivided into four plus three. Initially, to read something in this rhythm is to enter a state of confusion. For novices I opted to write it in 7/4, with bowings that emphasize the subdivision of each measure. In other words, there are actually two measures of 7/8 in each measure of 7/4. This rhythm is basic to a folk couples dance called the *ruchenitsa*.

"Sending the Bride to a Stranger's House" is based on a Russian folk theme in 5/4, which also appealed to the composer Rimsky-Korsakov. (He transcribed the original song, "The Bride's Farewell," for women's chorus.) My score is greatly transformed in melody and harmony but faithful in mood to this wedding-eve song, which dates from the time of stolen and bought brides. I gave the first violin the voice of the departing bride. The second violin is the voice of, perhaps, a resigned parent; it ends with a quote from John Coltrane's jazz tune "A Love Supreme."

Sending the Bride to a Stranger's House

By Hollis Taylor

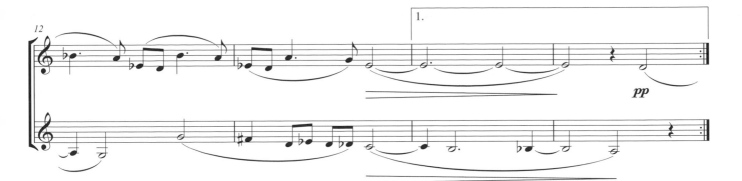

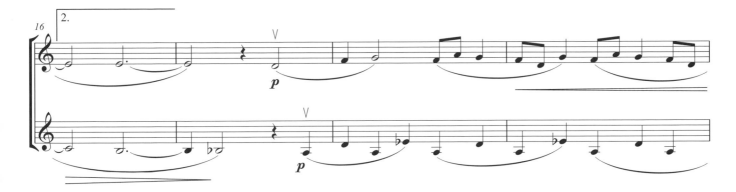

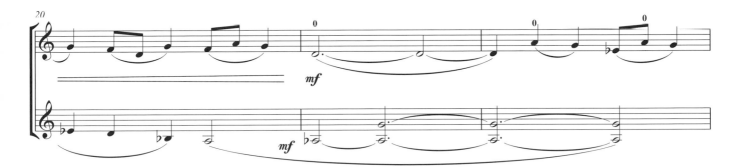

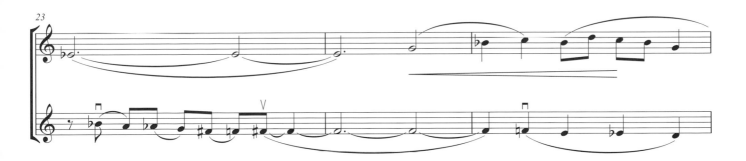

My musical travels also netted a Turkish tune in 9/4, mountain gavottes from Brittany in 21/8, and the meters 11/8 from Slovenia, 7/16 from Moldova, and 10/8 from Romania. It's been a dizzying experience. I stopped at nineteen tunes, leaving lots more rhythms to explore.

Unsquare Dances is available on CD and cassette, and in print scored for two violins or two violas.

BeauSoleil's "Chanson pour Tommy"

16

By Hollis Taylor

AMERICA'S PREMIER Cajun band, BeauSoleil, won a 1998 GRAMMY® for Best Traditional Folk Album for *L'Amour ou La Folie*. The latest release, *Cajunization* (Rhino, R2 75633), comes from the same kitchen. For this most recent pot of BeauSoleil gumbo, you start with the ever-present soulful Cajun French lyrics, hot fiddle licks, and irresistible accordion. Then you add the savory elements from different musical genres, including blues, surf, and Hawaiian, plus a dash of New Orleans jazz, a pinch of Caribbean rhythm, and a dollop of Old World ballads. The recipe varies from disc to disc, but the result is always hot and tasty.

BeauSoleil founder, fiddler, songwriter, and lead vocalist Michael Doucet is the descendant of French-speaking Acadians who settled in Nova Scotia in 1604. Their New World community was overturned in a 1755 event called *Le Grand Derangement*, when English soldiers seized the Acadians, arbitrarily splitting up families and forcing them onto ships sailing south. Half died on the voyage, while the survivors made their way to the protective isolation of Louisiana's bayous.

Doucet grew up speaking French at home, an influence that even the Americanization of his school days could not water down. He spent years studying the traditional music of the vanishing older generation of musicians. "I couldn't be doing what I'm doing if I hadn't learned a hundred songs by Dennis McGee," Doucet explains. "The more songs you play by these artists, the more you learn. First you understand their musical theories, then you can create music that fits within the tradition."

Doucet wrote both music and lyrics to a dozen new songs, as well as the lyrics to a pair of tracks composed by the late, great Cajun fiddler McGee. Then he wrote a track-by-track commentary and English translations. His fiddling is based on a "less is more" approach, and it always makes you dance, if only in your chair.

One of my favorites on the new recording is called "Chanson pour Tommy," dedicated to the late Dr. Tommy Comeaux, a member of BeauSoleil and other Acadian-based bands. A multi-instrumentalist and pathologist, his life was cut short in a tragic bicycling accident last year. (An all-star live disc featuring highlights from last year's tribute concert to Comeaux is available. Proceeds will be used to endow a chair at the University of Southwestern Louisiana to support traditional arts through scholarship, instruction, and community performances.)

The tune is played in two parts. First is a lilting waltz (all pairs of eighth notes should swing: the first should be longer in duration than the second). The waltz concludes with a distinct pause, and then the drummer begins a two-beat rhythm and the soloists crank up again, soloing one by one on this second theme, an adaptation of an old Acadian ballad that Comeaux brought to BeauSoleil.

BeauSoleil founder and fiddler Michael Doucet.

Chanson pour Tommy

Transcribed by Hollis Taylor

Solo #1

Solo #2

BEAUSOLEIL'S "CHANSON POUR TOMMY"

I sent Doucet an e-mail about "Chanson pour Tommy." "Do you have music written for it?" I asked. "If not, it's not a problem to transcribe it."

"Written?" came his reply. "Surely you jest..."

I then asked what readers should know about this tune. "As you can tell, it is a sad theme," Doucet answered. "Kind of like rewinding your thoughts of a happy event in your life that you cannot relive anymore, something precious has been taken away from you, and with musical brush strokes you recreate it. It's a waltz, which does bring those emotions out."

The entire tune could be played in double-stops, most of which can be made by bowing adjacent open strings. This technique is also called droning, or droning an open string. Example 1, at the end of the main tune, is a possible double-stop treatment of measures 13–16 of Solo #1.

Example 1

Yet another variation comes when BeauSoleil adds a second fiddle to the tune. The part consists of low double-stops based on chord tones that complement the overall resonance and enhance the rhythm without drawing attention to themselves. Example 2 gives the second fiddle part for measures 1–16 of Solo #1.

Example 2

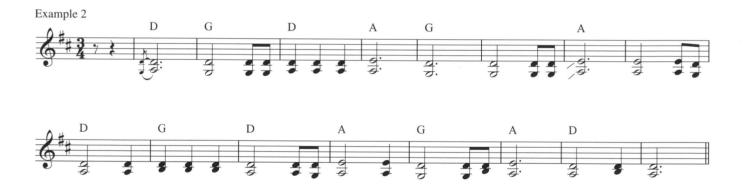

"Charles Sawtelle, our producer, just died after a long bout with leukemia," Doucet told me. "It was his idea to start out the song with fiddles. It's a little hard to play that tune now. But then, you go on and celebrate.

"I gave Tommy a tape of some old Cajun 78s and he liked this ballad, albeit at a faster tempo. We played it together for years but never recorded it, and it just seemed to fit the rejoicing mood and celebrate the good times. I'm just really sorry he wasn't there to play it."

I wondered if the switch from 3/4 to ₡ (measure 35) is common in Cajun music. "I never even thought about the time change, just the mood," said Doucet. "Kind of in the fashion of a New Orleans funeral: OK, you gotta bury your best friend, but then you gotta go on and celebrate the good times with a new spirit!"

Doucet also commented about how making music for dancers affects his playing. "That's the pulse of our music, to see people moving to the spirit of the moment, where music takes over the right side of the brain and we all come into contact with the same sound source that moves us involuntarily. We sense that, and all of a sudden our ability as musicians takes a leap and we are pushed into a different realm, either an improvised or time-traveled cadenza where we lock into something beyond our logical, everyday boundaries."

Contributors

Donna Hebért studied classical violin, sharing a stand with Elmar Oliveira in high school in Connecticut. At age 23 she converted to folk music and started fiddling, winning awards as one of the founders of the New England contradance renaissance. She has inaugurated "Fiddling for Violinists" seminars and courses with Connecticut-based string teacher Janet Farrar Royce and fiddling scholar Stacy Phillips.

Julie Lyonn Lieberman is an improvising violinist, singer, composer, educator, recording artist, author, and producer. Formerly on faculty at Juilliard, New York University, and The New School University's Jazz Program, she now teaches privately in her NYC studio. Lieberman is the author of seven books, instructional videos, and more than 55 articles for music-related publications.

Violinist **Fred Palmer** is a retired Professor of Music at Southern Oregon State College.

Stacy Phillips is a violinist and dobroist. He has written 15 books, including *The Complete Country Fiddler*, and the two-volume *Phillips Collection of Traditional American Fiddle Tunes*, published by Mel Bay.

James Reel is a freelance writer and editor covering the arts, literature, and border issues for the *National Catholic Reporter*, the *All Music Guide*, and NewMusicBox. Formerly, he was the editor of the *Tucson Weekly* and classical music critic and arts/entertainment editor at the *Arizona Daily Star*. Reel is a contributing editor for *Strings*, and has recently taken up the cello.

Pat Talbert: Chapter 2, "Bridging the Gap Between Classical and Traditional Music."

Hollis Taylor is a violinist/composer who composed her CD, *Unsquare Dances*, while residing in Budapest.

Fiddler **Suzy Rothfield Thompson** has performed with many top names in Cajun music, including the Savoy-Doucet Band, D.L. Menard, BeauSoleil, and Queen Ida. In the early 1980s she apprenticed with master fiddler Dewey Balfa in Louisiana under an NEA grant. She performed with the California Cajun Orchestra for its entire eighteen-year run, and can be heard on the orchestra's award-winning Arhoolie CDs. She performs with the Bluegrass Intentions.

Fiddler **Vivian Williams** has performed with several bluegrass bands and at numerous festivals, shows, colleges, dances, and on television and radio. She was editor of the *Seattle Folklore Society Journal* for nine years, and holds a masters degree in ethnomusicology.

Multi-instrumentalist **Jim Wood** works as a producer and instructor and performs with his wife, Inge. A fiddler since the age of ten, he is the five-time Tennessee state fiddle champion. He has recorded and performed with Ray Price, Emmylou Harris, John Hartford, John McEuen, and Roy Acuff. Wood also owns and operates his own recording studio. He has provided music for TNN, HBO, ESPN, and the Discovery Channel.

Hal Leonard Presents Guitar Instruction from

STRING LETTER PUBLISHING

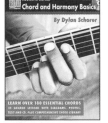

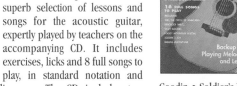

Hal Leonard Proudly Presents Guitar Reference Books from

S T R I N G   L E T T E R   P U B L I S H I N G

ACOUSTIC GUITAR OWNER'S MANUAL

Acoustic guitarists can now better understand their instruments, preserve and protect their value, and get the sounds they really want, thanks to this new book from the experts at *Acoustic Guitar* magazine. This indispensable guide begins by acquainting players with their instruments and laying to rest some pervasive guitar myths, then proceeds through various aspects of basic care, setup, common repairs, and pickup installation. Whether it's cleaning and polishing a beloved guitar, protecting it from theft or changes in humidity, selecting a case, or performing diagnostics, readers will become more savvy acoustic guitar owners and repair-shop customers and can forego dubious advice from well-meaning friends and anonymous "experts" on the Web. Includes a primer and glossary of terms.

_____00330532 (96 pages, 9" x 12") $17.95

ACOUSTIC GUITAR MAGAZINE'S BEST PRIVATE LESSONS

Players of all levels will relish this comprehensive and noteworthy collection of *Acoustic Guitar's* finest lessons. Here, at last, is an opportunity to explore a wide range of techniques, including fingerstyle, flatpicking, alternate tunings and bottleneck slide, while enjoying a variety of musical styles – rock, blues, Celtic, swing, bluegrass and more. You'll also learn how to make the most of your practice time, choose a teacher, and train your ear from the best guitar teachers around.

_____00695603 (80 pages, 9" x 12") $14.95

CLASSICAL GUITAR ANSWER BOOK
by Sharon Isbin

In this update of the *Acoustic Guitar Answer Book*, Sharon Isbin, the classical guitar virtuoso who heads the Juilliard School Guitar Department, answers 50 essential questions about performing, practicing, and choosing and caring for your guitar. The questions were asked by *Acoustic Guitar* magazine readers and answered by Isbin in four years of Master Class columns in the magazine; this book collects all this vital information together in an easy reference format – an absolute must for every classical guitar player. Includes new appendices of resources for classical guitarists and students.

_____00330443 (88 pages, 9" x 12") $14.95

CUSTOM GUITARS
A COMPLETE GUIDE TO CONTEMPORARY HANDCRAFTED GUITARS

This beautiful book is a comprehensive guide to the new Golden Age of handcrafted acoustic guitars! Illustrated with full-color photos of custom instruments throughout, this rich resource also contains profiles of top luthiers, advice on buying a custom instrument, and an extensive directory with complete contact information for hundreds of makers. Encompassing steel-string flattops, nylon-strings, resonators & Hawaiians, archtops and more, *Custom Guitars* presents the history and current state of the art of guitar making. Includes an intro by Alex de Grassi.

_____00330564 (150 pages, 9" x 12") $39.95

PERFORMING ACOUSTIC MUSIC
THE COMPLETE GUIDE

Whether you're a solo performer or a member of a band, stepping on stage for the first time or already building a career, gigging for money or just for the thrill of it, *Performing Acoustic Music* is the one complete guide to the art of successfully bringing your music to live audiences. In these pages, you'll find expert advice from top acoustic artists (including Suzanne Vega, Christ Proctor, Leo Kottke, Sharon Isbin, and more), as well as the sound engineers who set the stage and work the board. They learned it the hard way, and now their stories and insights will help you achieve success as a performer! From the publishers of *Acoustic Guitar* magazine.

_____00695512 (104 pages, 9" x 12") $14.95

ROCK TROUBADOURS
by Jeffrey Pepper Rodgers
Acoustic Guitar Backstage Series

In these revealing conversations, today's top artists offer a look inside their creative process as songwriters, guitarists, recording artists and performers. Includes Jerry Garcia and David Grisman, Paul Simon, Joni Mitchell, James Taylor, Ani DiFranco, Dave Matthews and Tim Reynolds, Indigo Girls, Ben Harper, Chris Whitley and more.

_____00330752 (128 pages, 6" x 9") $14.95

ROOTS & BLUES FINGERSTYLE GUITAR
by Steve James
Acoustic Guitar Private Lessons

Steve James presents a treasure trove of traditional American guitar styles in this unique book/CD pack. Guitarists will learn fingerpicking and slide techniques not through dry exercises but by playing 25 songs from James' own repertoire and from such masters as Furry Lewis, Blind Willie McTell, Sam McGee, and Mance Lipscomb. Drawing on his extensive research and first-hand experience with these guitar pioneers, James tells the stories behind the songs, too. Songs: Take Me Back • Sugar Babe • Milwaukee Blues • Sebastopol• John Henry • more! Includes tablature.

_____00699214 (96 pages, 9" x 12") $19.95

SONGWRITING AND THE GUITAR
THE COMPLETE GUIDE

With this unique and informative guide, you'll discover new ideas and inspirations for crafting your own songs and making the most of your instrument. You'll gain a better understanding of chord progressions, melodies, alternate tunings and other subjects through a series of expertly designed workshops, and you'll find tips and techniques offered by top singer-songwriters, such as Paul Simon, James Taylor, Joni Mitchell, Don McLean, Patty Larkin, David Wilcox, Dave Matthews and more.

_____00330565 (88 pages, 9" x 12") $14.95

VINTAGE GUITARS
THE INSTRUMENTS, THE PLAYERS, AND THE MUSIC

Vintage Guitars: The Instruments, the Players, and the Music is the first pictorial reference work to offer guitar enthusiasts, players and collectors an opportunity to explore the eventful, endless give-and-take between musicians and instrument makers that has produced America's popular music and its quintessential instrument. Generously illustrated with more than 150 photos of players, instruments, catalog pages and other memorabilia, this book features everything from the elegant American guitars of the 19th century to the evolving dreadnought, jumbo, 12-string, archtop resophonic and more – original instruments as well as contemporary incarnations and reissues. It spotlights the guitars of Leadbelly, Jimmie Rodgers, the Everly Brothers, Tony Rice, Emmylou Harris, Ben Harper and others. The collector's edition features the book in a classy, hard-back slip case.

_____00330780 (162 pages, 9" x 12") $39.95

FOR MORE INFORMATION, SEE YOUR LOCAL MUSIC DEALER,
OR WRITE TO:

7777 W. BLUEMOUND RD. P.O. BOX 13819 MILWAUKEE, WI 53213

Visit Hal Leonard Online at **www.halleonard.com**

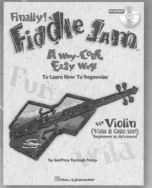
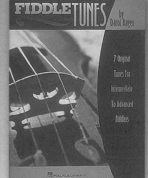

Hal Leonard Proudly Presents Reference Books from

S T R I N G   L E T T E R   P U B L I S H I N G

A CELLIST'S LIFE

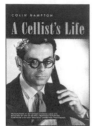

Strings Backstage Series

One of the 20th century's most distinguished cellists, Colin Hampton, is your guide to a bygone world of classical music and musicians. Through his witty, convivial, and candid narratives, you'll also encounter such luminaries as Pablo Casala, Ernest Bloch, Igor Stravinsky, Arturo Toscanini, Béla Bartók, Yehudi Menuhin, and other as never before.

_____00330753 (128 pages, 6" x 9") $12.95

ROCK TROUBADOURS

by Jeffrey Pepper Rodgers
Acoustic Guitar Backstage Series

In these revealing conversations, today's top artists offer a look inside their creative process as songwriters, guitarists, recording artists and performers. Includes Jerry Garcia and David Grisman, Paul Simon, Joni Mitchell, James Taylor, Ani DiFranco, Dave Matthews and Tim Reynolds, Indigo Girls, Ben Harper, Chris Whitley and more.

_____00330752 (128 pages, 6" x 9") $14.95

21ST-CENTURY CELLISTS

Strings Backstage Series

This collection of interviews sparkles with the individual personalities of some of this century's most gifted cellists. With voices as unique as their instruments', these musicians reveal the facets and textures of their professional and personal lives. From the intrepid Bion Tsang to the dynamic Kenneth Slowik and the charming Yo-Yo Ma, these artists and many others discuss what it's like to be a soloist, member of an ensemble, composer, mentor, musical activist and recording artist. How they began, what cultural and historical forces shaped them, how they practice, and what they aspire to – this and more are illuminated in this fascinating volume. Artists include: David Finckel, Ralph Kirshbaum, Laurence Lesser, Yo-Yo Ma, Kermit Moore, Carlos Prieto, Hai-Ye Ni, Kenneth Slowik, Bion Tsang, Jian Wang and Peter Wispelwey.

_____00330754 (128 pages, 6" x 9") $14.95

21ST CENTURY STRING QUARTETS, VOL.1

Strings Backstage Series

In this collection of in-depth interviews from the publishers of *Strings* magazine, some of the most talented and inspiring string quartets of our time explain how they work through their personal and musical relationships, from the practice room to the stage.

_____00330530 (128 pages, 6" x 9") $12.95

21ST CENTURY VIOLINISTS, VOLUME 1

Strings Backstage Series

A rare glimpse into the fascinating lives of classical violin soloists: how they practice, how they work with other musicians, their performance secrets and anxieties, what moves and inspires them – all this and more comes to life in this series of revealing one-on-one interviews with the writers of *Strings* magazine.

_____00699221 (128 pages, 6" x 9") $12.95

VIOLIN OWNER'S MANUAL

Here's the book that should have come with your violin! Written by a team of leading instrument makers, repairers and musicians, this is the one comprehensive guide to selecting, understanding, preserving and protecting any violin, from a modest fiddle to a priceless Stradivari. Richly illustrated with photographs and drawings, it covers topics including: selecting the proper instrument and bow, understanding common repairs, finding the right maker, guarding against theft, getting a good setup, protecting your violin, choosing a case, and more.

_____00330762 (152 pages, 6" x 9") $14.95

VIOLIN VIRTUOSOS

Strings Backstage Series

An exceptional variety of dynamic violin soloists are making their mark on the world's stages. *Violin Virtuosos* takes you into their world. In these compelling profiles, each musician reveals the personal, technical, and psychological aspects of their lives in music: how they cope with isolation, how they approach and interpret their repertoire, and what kindles their passions and unites them with their audiences. This fascinating companion to Vol. 1 includes profiles of Joshua Bell, Vadim Repin, Kyung-Wha Chung, Hilary Hahn, Viktoria Mullova, Leila Josefowicz, Christian Tetzlaff and more.

_____00330566 (128 pages, 6" x 9") $12.95

HEALTHY STRING PLAYING

PHYSICAL WELLNESS TIPS FROM THE PAGES OF *STRINGS* MAGAZINE

Whether it's coping with overuse problems, conquering performance anxiety, or just keeping your body in great string-playing shape, experts from the pages of *Strings* magazine will help you in all areas of player wellness. This handy guide includes helpful tips from performers, teachers, students, and doctors to keep you playing at your best.

_____00695955 (160 pages, 6" x 9") $14.95

MAKING YOUR LIVING AS A STRING PLAYER

CAREER GUIDANCE FROM THE EXPERTS AT *STRINGS* MAGAZINE
edited by Greg Cahill

Inside this volume, culled from the pages of the award-winning *Strings* magazine, you will find practical tips on writing a résumé, starting a freelance career, creating your own chamber music series, setting up a successful teaching studio in your home, and much, much more to help you jumpstart your career as a professional string player.

_____00331094 (96 pages, 6" x 9") $12.95

MAKING A MUSICAL LIFE

THE PRACTICE, THE PROFESSION, THE JOY
by Tom Heimberg

Tom Heimberg draws upon decades of experience in the orchestra pit and the teaching studio to provide a practical and engaging look at living the life of a professional musician. Musicians and music lovers of all levels will appreciate the wealth of practical information this book provides, interwoven with humorous vignettes about working and playing with inspired musicians of the 20th century.

_____00331748 (130 pages, 6" x 9") $14.95

Prices, contents, and availability subject to change without notice.

FOR MORE INFORMATION, SEE YOUR LOCAL MUSIC DEALER, OR WRITE TO:

7777 W. BLUEMOUND RD. P.O. BOX 13819 MILWAUKEE, WI 53213

Visit Hal Leonard Online at **www.halleonard.com**

0407